HANCOCK COUNTY GEORGIA

Inferior Court Minutes

- 1800-1808

(Volume #1)

Compiled by:
Michael A. Ports

Southern Historical Press, Inc.
Greenville, South Carolina

Copyright 2019
By: Michael A. Ports

All rights reserved. No part of this publication may be reproduced, stored in a retrieval system, transmitted in any form, posted on to the web in any form or by any means without the prior written permission of the publisher.

Please direct all correspondence and orders to:

www.southernhistoricalpress.com
or
SOUTHERN HISTORICAL PRESS, Inc.
PO BOX 1267
375 West Broad Street
Greenville, SC 29601
southernhistoricalpress@gmail.com

ISBN #0-89308-835-8

Printed in the United States of America

Introduction

The Georgia General Assembly created Hancock County on December 17, 1793, from parts of Greene and Washington counties, and established Sparta as the seat of its government. Part of Baldwin County, east of the Oconee River, was part of Hancock County prior to 1807. A portion of Hancock County was taken to form Taliaferro County in 1825. The Inferior Court, comprised of five elected justices of the peace for the county, tried any civil case, except those involving title to land. The Inferior Court had jurisdiction over all county business matters, such as care for the poor, building and maintaining the courthouse and jail, building and maintaining public roads, bridges, and ferries, issuing licenses to sell liquor, nominating justices of the peace, performing naturalizations, appointing guardians, authorizing apprenticeships and indentures, and administering county funds.

The folllowing transcription is taken from the microfilm made at the county courthouse in Sparta on December 29, 1960 by the Genealogical Society of Salt Lake City, Utah and is available at the Georgia Archives in Morrow, Georgia and the Family History Library. The heading on the microfilm roll treads

State of Georgia

Hancock County

Inferior Court

Minutes

County Purposes

Book 1800 – 1808

Index No

The minutes commence on July 12, 1800 and continue through November 7, 1808. On the inside front cover, the clerk wrote

1800
1808
Inf Ct
Min
Co Purposes

At the top of the first page, the clerk wrote

County Minutes 1800 to 1808

The first volume of original court minutes is not indexed; however, a complete full-name index follows the transcription. The reader should know that a lone surname in the index indicates that no first name appears in the minutes, for example Mr. Smith, Smith & Company, or said Smith. An index entry such as Smith, ___, Sm___, William, or ___, William indicates that an entire name was entered into the minutes, but at least part of it has been obscured by an ink blot, smear, tear, or other imperfection. The clerk numbered nearly all of the original pages, but stopped doing so after page number 261. Thereafter, to assist the researcher in locating the original pages, the symbol ___ is placed at the bottom left-hand corner of each original unnumbered page. By noting the date, or at least the court term, of an individual entry in the minutes, the researcher should not have too much difficulty in locating that entry in the original record or on the microfilm copy.

Bolling Hall, Martin Martin, and James Lewis served as clerk during the period covered by the minutes. In addition, Alexander Martin and Frederick Freeman substituted for the clerk at various times. The clerk usually signed the minutes at the close of each day's proceedings, attesting to their accuracy. Based upon the different handwriting, at least two others entered some of the daily proceedings, but their names were not recorded. For the most part, their handwriting is legible, making the transcription straightforward and not too difficult. The occasional ink smear or other imperfection is noted within brackets, for example [smear], [torn], or [illegible]. The transcription follows Sperry's recommended guidelines for reading early American script.[1]

Sometimes the clerks formed the letters "a" and "o" in a very similar manner, making abbreviations such as Jas. and Jos. and sunames Harman and Harmon or Low and Law impossible to distinguish. At other times, the letters "a" and "u"

---

[1] Sperry, Kip. *Reading Early American Handwriting.* Genealogical Publishing Company, Inc., Baltimore, Maryland, Sixth Printing, 2008.

are too similar to differentiate between such names as Burnett and Barnett. The formation of the letters "i" and "e" sometimes makes it difficult to distinguish between such names as Melton and Milton, for example. Also, the clerk formed the capital letters "I" and "J" identically. Determining which letter usually is not a problem when the first letter of a surname, but entirely a guess when a middle initial. Sometimes the clerk crossed the letter "t" by extending the horizontal line across the entire word, making it difficult to distinguish between such surnames as Cutter, Cutler, and Culter or Cotton and Colton. Occasionally, the clerk failed to cross the letter "t" at all, leaving the reader wondering if the name was Jewett or Jewell, for example.

The transcription does not correct any grammar or spelling, no matter how obvious the errors, but does add a few commas, semicolons, apostrophes, and periods for clarity. Finally, the clerk entered a vertical squiggly line to delineate case citations and other headings, duplicated by the symbol } in the transcription. Careful researchers will consult either the original record or the microfilm copy either to confirm the transcription or formulate alternative interpretations of the clerks' handwriting.

Generally, the transcription maintains the overall format of the minutes, but presents the case citations, jury panels, lists of witnesses, and other court proceedings in a standard and consistent format. The minutes contain numerous original signatures, beyond merely those of the judge and the clerk, including those of many attorneys, individuals filing bonds for appeals and stays of execution, and their securities, as well as those subscribing to various oaths.

The book is dedicated to the memory of the author's numerous Georgia ancestors, although none ever were residents of Hancock County. Many thanks are offered to the kind, patient, and generous staff of the Georgia Archives, for their assistance and suggestions, not only in locating the original records, but in understanding their historical context. Thanks also are offered LaBruce Lucas of the Southern Historical Press for his sage professional advice and counsel. Special thanks are offered to my mother, Ouida J. Ports, who helped instill in me a deep appreciation of American history and genealogy.

Inferior Court Minutes

Georgia Hancock County [1]

At an adjourned Court began and held for the State and County aforesaid On the 12th day of July 1800.

> Present their Honors   Risdon Moore }
> Anderson Comer } Esq^{rs}
> Andrew Baxter }
> Henry Graybill }

Ordered

N^o (1) That the Road from Obadiah Richardson's to Powelton compose one district and that the following persons work thereon, Viz.

John Cooper, Thomas Weeks, William Ousley, Joseph Cooper, Sn^r, Needham Jernigan, Sn^r, Joseph Henry, Jarard Burch, Aaron Woodward, John Colbert, & Jesse Connel, Oversear.

(2) The Second district including the new Road from where it leaves the Greensborough Road to Shoulderbone at Doct^r S. Acee's plantation, the following persons to work thereon, Viz.

Henry Miller, Nathan Clay, Housdon Mapp, Henry Jackson, Stephen Jackson, Isaac Jackson, Isaac Jackson, Sn^r, David Jackson, Peter Dent, Isaac Newton, John Moreland, Richd Moore, Jacob Mason, William Moon, James Barnes, Nathan Barnes, John Dickinson, John Caldwell, Ja[blot] Caldwell, William Caldwell, Henry Dickinson, Thomas Hickinbottom, William Reese, Josiah Beall, William C. Barksdale, Saml Dent, Robert Holt, Michael Gilbert, Plesent Moman, Epaphroditus Drake, William Lawson, Sn^r, & Joseph Hickinbottom, Oversear.

12th July 1800 [2]

N^o (3) That the third district shall include the Road from Shoulderbone at Doct^r S. Acee's plantation to Thaddeus Holt's, the following persons to work thereon, Viz.

Ephraim Barnes, William Lawson, ju^r, Thomas Cates, William Wright, George Parker, Nathan Daniel, William Barnes, Jesse Maddox, Ralph Low, Henry

Colquitt, Saml Person, Jethro Barnes, William Twilla, Joseph [faint], Francis Richardson, Joshua Kinney, Peter Merrel, Thaddeus Holt, Tapley Holt, & Absalom Barnes, Oversear. iss^d

4 That the fourth district shall include the road from Obadiah Richardson's to Joseph Thomas's on the Academy, on which the following Hands shall work, Viz.

Obadiah Richardson, Davis McGehee, Robert Gilmore, Samuel Maddox, Isaac Benson, John Sperling, John Culver, Revd John Thomas, James Beach, William Bullock, Sarah Thomas, Phlaner Shores, Singleton Holt, Britton Emerson, Samuel Twilla, Risdon Moore, jn^r, Oversear. iss^d

(5) That the fifth district shall include the Road from Obadiah Richardson's to Martin Gilbert's, & the following Persons to work thereon, Viz.

William Dent, jn^r, William Dent, Sn^r, Risdon Moore, Sn^r, Zachariah Middleton, Hines Holt, Bolling Hall, John & Solomon Lankston, Wyche & Tisdal Whatley, Abner Barksdale, Taylor Nelson, John Hill, & ~~Philip Alen~~, Jo^s Barksdale, Oversear. iss^d

[pages 3 and 4 missing and not filmed]

12th July 1800   [5]

Ordered, That the Oversears of the different Roads be requested to make and return Correct lists of the hands liable to work on the Road within their respective districts to the next adjourned Court. iss^d

Ordered, That a Road be laid out and Opened from the Academy Lands on Shoulderbone leading the nearest & best way to Strike the Greensborough Road near the Widdow Middleton's House, thence the nearest & best Way to intersect a Road leading to Powelton, near Henry Graybill's plantation, & that Josiah Beale, Robert Holt, & Samuel Dent be Commissioners & William C. Barksdale Oversear to carry the same into effect. iss^d

Ordered, that the Sum of twenty eight dollars and fifty Cents be appropriated and paid to Samuel Hale, also the sum of five dollars & fifty cents in full for his services as the Jaylor of Hancock County. $34 appr^d Paid

Ordered, That Joseph Hambrick, Orphan of Thomas Hambrick, be bound and apprenticed to Edward Bazer untill the 24th day of March 1805, he then being twenty one years of age, also that Edward Bazer be appointed his guardian, and that he enter into bond of four hundred dollars with Samuel Barron & Nathan Saunders, Security.

12th July 1800 [6]

Rec^d of William Devereux, Esqr four dollars & Eighty one and a quarter cents for estrays sold by him. 4.81¼

Rec^d of John Crowder, Esqr the sum of twenty eight dollars for Estrays sold by him. 28

Ordered, that Ephraim Moore, Esqr & Arthur Danielly be appointed Oversear of the Road from town Creek to Montpelier & that they divide and apportion the hands as equally as may be and return a list of the same to the next adjourned court. Iss^d

Ordered, that the sum of two Dollars & fifty cents be paid to James Thomas for the use of Mrs Walker in full for the appropriation for 1798. 2.50 paid

Ordered, That Absolom Eilans, William Carter, & John Armstrong, Esq^{rs} be and they are hereby appointed Commissioners to lay out a Road from Eilands's Mill on Buffaloe to the road leading from the whitebluff, & that Swan Thompson be appointed Oversear to open & keep the same in Repair. Iss^d

Ordered, That the Road leading from the Cedar Shoals on the Oconee to Sparta from John Ragan's, Esq^{rs} ~~shall compose the tenth district~~ to Nathaniel Waller's shall compose the 10th district, & the following Hands shall

12 July 1800 [7]

Work thereon, Viz.

Dis^t N° 10. Hardy Smith, John Reid, Chas McDonald, James McCormac, Thomas Wynn, John Roe, Henry Bond, Joseph Buttrage, John Barron, Matthew Derham, Jacob Powel, Benjamin Bott, Jamison Comer, Solomon Thornton, Elisha Ellis, John Bond, Joseph Strickland, Thomas Strickland, Robert Strickland, Isham Smith, John Smith, Nathan Henryton, John Humphries, Eli Tool, Matthew Dennis, Lindsy Thornton, Simon Brewer, Saml Barron, & that Hardy Smith be Oversear. iss^d

(11) That the Road leading from Logdam to Fort creek sall Compose the 11th district and the following hands shall work thereon

Hubbard Browne, William Browne, Anderson Comer, James Comer, James Ross, James Grace, Jonathan Hosey, John Wedington, William Hudson, Danl Melson, Quinney Pope, Ephraim West, Richard Fulwell, John Purify, Presley Ingram, John Sturdivant, John Hudman, John Vest, Jonathan McKisie, John Roe, Robt Finch, Ja^s Murphey, John Hamlin, James Browne, Edward Butler, Joseph Butridge, Richardson Black, & Mark Jackson, Oversear. iss^d

(12) That the Road leading from Fulsom's ford on Ogechee River to dry creek near Henry Bankston's Compose the 12th district, and the following hands shall work thereon, viz.

Martin Powel, George Fenn, Solomon Barfield, John Latimer, Mark Gonder, Hezekiah Howell, Francis Griffin, Lewis Tannin, Dempsy Griffin, James Humphrey, Matthew Humphrey, Thos Humphrey, Philip Hargrove, Thomas Saterwhite, John Williams, Jeremiah Long, William Willis, Thos Willis, James Miller, j^r, John Harrison, j^r, Wm Horn, Thos Miller, John Gibson, William Sheffield, & Henry Bankston, Oversear. iss^d

12th July 1800 [8]

Dis^t N^o (13) That the Road leading from Montpelier to Greensborough, from Thomas Lloyd's to to Fort Creek compose the 13th Dis^t, and that the following hands work thereon, Viz.

John Simmons, Nathan Saunders, Abraham Wamack, William Wamack, Thomas Wynn, Sn^r, Joshua Wynn, Stephen Kirk, James Hale, Mark Saunders, Zorobabel Williamson, Bryan Stonham, James Stoneham, & Henry Tripp, oversear. issued

14 That the road leading from Lewisville, between the Georgetown Road near Edmond Beard's and Benjamin Avrett's at the cross Roads compose the 14th Dis^t, and that the following hands work thereon, viz.

John Peace, William Grantham, [blank] Adkinson, Joshua Grayham, [blank] Grayham, James Majors, James Walker, Alexander Walker, Robt Montgomery, William John, Nathaniel Parham, John Browne, Allen Browne, William Gilliland, John Browne, Starling Almonds, Joseph Herndon, & John Perkins, Over Sear. iss^d

15th That the Road leading from Sparta to Chambers' Mill from the Stoney Hill Compose the 15th district, & that the following hands work thereon, viz.

William Evans, Caleb Kennedy, Isham Reese, Richard Respess, Saml Turner, Thomas Brantley, John Grammer, John Browne, James Onail, Ja^s Shackleford, Saml Reed, Alexander Reed, William Harper, Zadoc Stinson, Malachi Brantley, John Turner, Joseph Turner, John Broadnax, John Onail, Ed^w Taylor, Ja^s Morris, William Tripp, W^m McGaughey, Jno Tripp, Ja^s Reese, Thos Wilemon, Jo^s McGaughey, Is^h Greene, Shadrack Roe, Robt Chambers,

12th July 1800 [9]

Joseph Johnson, & John Gay, Oversear. iss^d

(16) That the Road from Broad Street in Sparta to George Cowen's compose the 16th Dis^t, & that the following hands work thereon

Brice Gaither, Ja^s Saunders, John Saunders, William Reese, James Huff, Lundy Huff, John Lucas's hands, James Hale, Joshua Betts, William Pride, Anderson Reese, Henry Brown, Robert Pollard, John T. Spencer, John Tatum, Martin Martin, & George Cowen, Oversear. Iss^d

(17) That the Road leading from Sparta to Montpelier, from where it leaves the Road which leads to Chambers' Mill, to Nathaniel Waller's Compose the 17th dis^t, & that the following hands work thereon, viz.

Wm Sallard, Job Tyson, John C. Peak, Willie Burge, John Hamilton, William Hamilton, Fred Equals, Henry Mitchell, John Crowder, Wm Thornton, Willie Smith, Edwd Bazer, William Bazer, John Staunton, John Maclemore, Henry Thornton, Epps Browne, Wyatt Collier, & Nathaniel Waller, Oversear. Iss^d

(18) That the Road from Sparta to Stith's Mill & fare as Barksdale's fork Compose the 18th Dis^t, & the following hands to work thereon, viz.

David Clements, Thomas Ford, James Jones, Saml Ewings, Jesse Veazey, Thomas Gordin, Richard Pounds, James Evans, Barnaby Shivers, William Gay, John Buckner, jn^r, Peter Saunders, Jeffry Barksdale, Jesse Allen, Abraham Hickman, John Matthews, Parham Buckner, John Thweatts, & James Huddleston, Oversear. Joel Buckner, John Buckner, Senr, Thomas Gay, Thomas Ewing, John Miller, Solomon Bankes, & Slade Durham added by inform^n. iss^d

12th July 1800 [10]

Dist No (19) That the Road leading from Joseph Thomas's to Chambers' Mill compose the 19th dist, and that the following hands work thereon, viz.

Erby Hudson, William Hudson, Thos Hudson, Moses Willis, Hezekiah Kindrick, Walter Hamilton, Gibble Thomas, David Dickson, William Palmer, William Reese, Andrew Baxter, & William Thomas, Oversear, also Jos Thomas. issd

20 That the Old Trail Road between Britton's old place & the cross Roads where Moses Harris formerly lived compose the 20th dist, & the following Hands work thereon, viz.

Hamlin Lewis, John Kirk, Joel Buckner, Willie Buckner, Benj Buckner, Robert Thornton, Widdow Duglass's hands, Frederick Tilman, Joel Pounds, David Pounds, & Allen Bird, Oversear. issd

[Vertically in the left margin next to the above entry, the clerk wrote, Discontinued 24th Feby 1801.]

21 That the Road leading from Georgetown from the old Washington County line to Little Ogechee Compose the 21st Dist, & the following hands work thereon, viz.

~~Benj Thompson~~, John Turner, Peter Boyle, Joab Durham, Willie Whatley, Edmond Baird, Francis Lewis, James Ward, Solomon Philips, Sanders Herring, Edward Denton, [blank] Copeland, Saml John, & James Page, oversear, also James Lewis, William Lewis, Shadrach Taylor, Hamlin Lewis, John [blot], Jesse Page, James Shy, James Castleberry, John Tilman, [smudge] Joel Patterson, Jonathan Thomas, [smudge] Turner, Parham Buckner, James Thorn, Da[faint] John, Benj Buckner, Isham Huckaby, & Benj Temple. issued

12th July 1800 [11]

Dist No 22 That the Road from Buffaloe at the Widdow Hunter's to Eilands's Mill Compose the 22nd Dist, & the following hands work thereon,

John Carter, Charles Johnson, James Bonner, Abraham Borland, John Cain, Job Jackson, Jacob Ernest, [blank] Johnson, John Lewis, Job Allen, Wm Saunders, Hillery Philips, William Harvey, Zephaniah Harvey, Darling Lewis, Alban Bailey, Wm Howard, David Irwin, Joseph Greene, [faint] Armstrong, Jas Jones, Tho Jones, Wm Cain, junr, Wm Carter, Jos Carter, Thos Carter, Jesse Carter,

Jonathan Nichols, Robt Stell, Zephaniah Harvey, Nehemiah Harvey, Jno Harvey, Wm Harvey, Thos Harvey, J. Barrentine Carter, [smudge] James Cain, Hillery Phillips, Overseer. iss^d

23 That the Road leading from Sparta to the Buffaloe Creek at the Widow Hunter's Compose the 23 Dis^t, & the following hands work thereon, viz.

William Reese, [blot] Richard Bonner, Richd Smith, Richd Gary, Ja^s Wilkinson, [blank] Wilkinson, Hubbard Bonner, Robert Rains, David Pinkerton, James Gary, Hartwell Gary, ~~Bath Wyches~~, Benjamin Thompson, Duke Hamilton, James Hamilton, & James Pinkston, Oversear. iss^d

24 That the road leading from Nathaniel Waller's to John Calhoun's Compose the 24th Dis^t, & that the following persons work thereon, viz.

Cader Powell, Thomas Vickars, William Smith, John Winslet, Alex Lyles, Drury Musslewhite, [blank] Musslewhite, William Piper, James Baswell, Jacob Dennis, John Dennis, Abram Peavey, James Works, Ja^s Scott, & Thos Lloyd, oversear. Iss^d

12th July 1800 [12]

25 That the Road leading through Sparta to the old Washington County line beginning at the Stoney Hill Compose the 25th Dis^t, & that the following persons work thereon, viz.

Charles Abercrombie, Lewis Moss, Epps Moss, Woodlief Scott, Thompson Bird, Timothy Rositer, Appleton Rositer, Joel Langbetter, John Howard, John Scott, Frederick Scott, Willie Abercrombie, John Lucas, Philip Turner, William Sanford, James Bogue, Joel Fric[blot] Simson Sollar, Richd Bryan, Isaac Bryan, William Stembridge, John Pinkston, John Comer, Alexander Long, John B. Devereux, & Saml Devereux, oversear.

Court then adjourned untill Second Saturday in August.

B. Hall, Clk   A. Comer
                                             Risdon Moore
                                             And^w Baxter
                                             Hen. Graybill

Hancock Inf' Court 6th October 1800 [13]

At a meeting of the Justices of the Inferior Court for County business.

Present their Honors   Henry Graybill }
                       Risdon Moore   } Esq^{rs}
                       Anderson Comer }

Ordered, That John Freeman, Epps Browne be And they are hereby ~~Authorised~~ appointed Inspectors of Tobacco in the town of Sparta at Clements's Warehous, and that Henry Moss be third inspector.

Ordered, that a Sum equal to one seventh part of the General Tax be levied and Collected by the tax Collector for the year 1800, Subject to the order of the Inferior Court.

Hancock Inf' Court 6th October 1800 [14]

Ordered, That Charles Abercrombie, Henry Moss, S^r, and Jn° W. Devereux be and they are hereby appointed Commissioners to let to the lowest bidder the painting of the Out Side the Court House, & doors and windows to be done in a Compleat workman like manner. issued

Ordered, that the different Collectors and persons having public money in their hands be prepared and ready for a Settlement at the next Inferior Court and that they present their acc^{ts} to Bolling Hall for examination.

John Harbirt & Andrew Baxter came on the bench.

Ordered, That Joel McClendon, George Lee, & John Miles be and they are hereby appointed Inspectors of Tob° at Montpelier warehouse.

	Risdon Moore
And^r Baxter	Hen. Graybill
John Harbirt	A. Comer

Court adjourned untill Court in Course.

B. Hall, Clk

Hancock Inferior Court 5th January 1801 [15]

Court met pursuant to adjournment.

Present their Honors Anderson Comer }
 Risdon Moore & } Esquires
 Andrew Baxter }

Ordered, That Joseph B. Chambers, Joseph Turner, & Henry Dixon be and they are hereby appointed Commissioners to view a road to lead from Thaddeus Holt's, round the plantation of said Joseph B. Chambers, to the Piney woods house, and make report thereof to the next Inferior Court.

Ordered, That William Hudson & Abner Lockett be appointed Overseers to open & lay out a road to lead from Joseph Cooper's mill on Logdam Creek to Sparta the nearest & best way.

The Court proceeded to open & hold an Election for receiver of tax returns & Collector of Taxes for the present year, & on counting out the ballots, it appeared that Hamlin Lewis was duly elected receiver of tax returns and Leonard Abercrombie Collector of taxes.

Moses

5th January 1801 [16]

Moses Marshall, having made satisfactory proof on oath to the Court, that a black Mare tolled by Mary Parker before John Harbirt, Esqr on the 10th January 1799 was his right & property, & the said Mare being sold as an Estray by the late Clerk of the Inferior Court. Ordered, that the sum of twenty seven dollars twenty Cents be paid by the Clerk to the applicant out of the money arising from the sale of Estrays, being the amount for which said Mare sold, after deducting the legal fees.

Ordered, that Peter Boyle, Hamlin Lewis, & Geoffery Barksdale, Esquires be authorized to lett to the lowest bidder the building of a bridge over Little Ogechee near Barksdale's Saw mill. issued

Ordered, that the Clerk do pay William Warthen, esq^r the sum of sixteen dollars twenty five Cents, being the am^t due from the County of Hancock for repairing the bridge across Ogechee near George Town. paid. J. Hamell, Esqr

5th January 1801 [17]

Ordered, that the Collector of taxes and all others holding public money or funds belonging to the County adjust their respective accounts and pay their several arrearages to the Clerk of this Court and that the Clerk do pay out all sums which may be appropriated & now due as far as he may be possessed of public money not otherwise appropriated.

Ordered, That John Miles be & he is hereby appointed a justice of the peace for Capt Yarborough's District in place of Joel McClendon, Esqr, resigned. Robert McGinty a justice of the peace in the place of Levi Daniel, deceased, in Capt Booth's district. And Joseph B. Chambers a justice of the peace in Capt Chambers' district, in place of Joseph Turner, resigned. issued

Ordered, that Samuel Parker be appointed Constable for Capt Yarborough's District, Jeremiah Walker for Capt Booth's District, Samuel Halley for Capt Williams' district,

5th January 1801 [18]

Matthew Durham Constable for Capt Bond's Dis^t, John Whitehurst Cons^l for Capt Reid's District, Noah Dodridge Cons^l for Capt Clark's District, Nicholas Dixon Cons^l for Capt Scott's District, Jesse Ellis Cons^l for Capt Chambers' District, James Orrick Cons^l for Capt Lucas' District, Ben^j Evans Cons^l for Capt Davis' Distric^t, James Davidson Cons^l for Capt Latimore's Dis^t, Th^o Hawkins Cons^l for Capt Dixon's District, Richard Garey Cons^l for Capt Barksdale's District, William Harvey Cons^l for Capt Carter's District, Arthur Youngblood Cons^l for Capt Mathews' District, & that the present Constable be continued for Capt Mason's District.

Ordered, that Saml McGehee & Cornelius Whittington be and they are hereby appointed commissioners to view & lay out a road leading from Joel McClendon's, Esqr down the Oconee to the line of Washington County the nearest & best way, and Joseph Porter be appointed oversear of said road, who is directed to return a list of hands liable to work thereon.

Issued

5th January 1801 [19]

Ordered, that Ephraim Moore, esquire & Arthur Danielly do notify the hands liable to work on the road leading from Town Creek to Montpellier warehouse, as apportioned by said Moore & Danielly, to compel their attendance as required by Law.

            Risdon Moore
            And^w Baxter
            A. Comer

Court then adjourned until the 23rd Feby next.

Attest. Mar Martin, Clk

At a meeting of the Justices of the Inferior Court for the County of [20] Hancock for County business on the 23rd day of February 1801.

Present, their Honors   Henry Graybill }
              Andrew Baxter } Esqrs
              Joel McClendon }

Ordered, that the sum of fifty four dollars be appropriated to the use of William Clark, a Parishoner, & paid to the oversears of the poor. paid.

Ordered, that the sum of thirty dollars be appropriated & paid to the oversears of the poor for the use of Mary Jasper, also the sum of thirty five dollars for the use of Mary Starn, also the Sum of thirty dollars for the use of Jesse Butler, & the Sum of Twenty dollars for the use of Thomas Smith, Parishoners. paid James Thomas $169.

Ordered, that the Sum of nineteen dollars ninety seven and three quarter Cents be appropriated to the use of Bolling Hall for services rendered the County, the balance due for him for County money in his hands.

Hancock Inf^r Court 23rd Feby 1801 [21]

Court adjourned untill tomorrow 10 o'Clock.

	Hen. Graybill
	And^w Baxter
B. Hall, Clk pro Tem	Joel McClendon

24th Feby 1801 Court met According to adjournment.

Present, their Honors   Henry Graybill }
                               Andrew Baxter   } Esq^{rs}
                               Joel McClendon }

26 Ordered, that the Road leading from the Pineywoods house to Georgetown, as fare as Augustin Morris's, Compose the 26th district, and that the following hands work thereon, Viz.

William Mangam, Joel Moody, Aaron Strauther, Richard Strauther, Ben^j Harper, Joseph Knowles, Abije Anderson, Chas Buckner, Thos Butler, Edward Turner, Benjamin Hearn, Thomas Hearn, Samuel Watts, West Jones, James Haynes, John Miller, Blacksmith, George Strauther, James McGehee, [blank] Graves, and that George Strauther, Oversear.

Hancock Inf^r Court Feby 1801 [22]

27 Ordered, That the Road leading from Sparta to Stith's Mill, from Barksdale's Fork to Fulsom's Creek, Compose the 27th district and the following hands to work thereon, viz.

William Harper, Thomas King, Darby Lary, Daniel Lary, John Dennis, Thomas Mason, George Allen, Jesse Allen, John Kelley, Chas Stewart, Daniel Browne, Jonathan Davis, Lemuel Davison, Samuel Barron, James Willson, Samuel Pope, Francis Langford, William Gay, William Andrews, Thos Willis, John Latimore, William Powell, Gabriel Moffet, John Harper, Berry Thomson, Jonathan Callaway, [smear] Bird, Robert Thornton, William Seals, Danl Seals, Spencer Seals, John Pound, Joel Pound, and Amos Brantley, Oversear. Issued.

Ordered, that the Road Composing the 21st district be turned from Edmond Beard's around the South side of Z. John's Plantation, the nearest and best way into the road leading from Sparta to Georgetown, and that James Thomas & James Page & Edmond Beard be appointed Commissioners to lay out the same. Issued.

Hancock Inf^r Court Feby 1801 [23]

28 Ordered, that the Road leading from Stith's Road to Fulsom's foard on Ogechee through Humphries' Lane, leaving the same between Saml Barron's & Ben^j Cook's, Compose the 28th district, and that the following hands work thereon, viz.

George Hays, Dempsy Hays, William Willis, ~~Thomas~~ John Gipson, Mesheck Howell, Gray Andrews, William Musgrove, John Wisenan, Thomas Humphries, Dempsy Griffin, Francis Griffin, Hezekiah Howell, Mark Gonder, Lewis Tanner, Jeremiah Lary, George Lary, Cecil Kemp, John Williams, Joseph Harrison, John Harrison, Ben^j Chapman, Richard Castleberry, William Shuffield, Thomas Harwell, Philip Rawles, Thomas Lovett, Richard Lovett, j^r, and James Miller, j^r, Oversear. Issued.

Ordered, That the Clerk at any time be authorised to enter any hands which may be returned to him by the Oversears of the different districts to the lists of hands liable to work on ~~thereon~~ the Road composing said district.

Ordered, That Ephraim Moore, Esqr, William Bivins, & Jesse Talbert be appointed Commissioners to let to the lowest bidder the building of a Bridge over Town Creek at Bivins's Mill, and that they take Bond from the undertaker with sufficient Security to keep the same in repair for five years.

Hancock Inf^r Court Feby 1801 [24]

29th Ordered, that the Road leading from ~~leading from~~ Cooper's Mill to Sparta, from Parham's Mill to the Sparta Road, Compose the 29th district, and that the following hands work thereon, viz.

Philip Pritchett, Wyatt Collier, Stith Parham, Jackson Harwell, James Thweatt, Jesse Grigg, Lewis Barnes, William Hamilton, Joshua Cuter, and Abner Lockett, Oversear. iss^d

Hen. Graybill
Joel McClendon
And^w Baxter

Court then adjourned untill the 1st day of June next.

B. Hall, Clk pro Tem

At an Inferior Court begun & held in & for the County of Hancock on [25]
Monday the 1st June 1801.

Present, their Honors   Anderson Comer }
                             Andrew Baxter }
                             Joel McClendon } Esquires
                             John Bailey   }

Ordered, That the sum of one hundred and twelve dollars be appropriated and paid to Jeffery Barksdale, in full for building a bridge over Little Ogechee near his Mill, agreeably to an Order of the Inferior Court. 27th Ap^l and June 1801. Rec^t p^d 4 Sep^r [faint]

Ordered, That the sum of fifty dollars be appropriated & paid to John Buckner, in part for painting the Court house. paid.

Ordered, That a Road be laid out the nearest and best way from the mouth of Shoulderbone to

to James Thweatt's, so as to cross Fort creek at Britain Rogers's, and [26]
join the road leading from Sparta to James Thweatt's at his plantation, that Britain Rogers, Francis Lewis, Junr, & John Smith be Commissioners from the mouth of Shoulderbone to Town creek & Joel Reese Overseer from Fort creek to James Thweatt's, and that the following hands work thereon, viz.

Britain Rogers, Burwell Rogers, John Lewis, Littleton Reese, Ransom Harwell, John Jackson, William Hurt, Alex^r Dunn, John Smith, Arch^d Smith, Joseph Westmoreland, Reuben Westmoreland, Mary Smith, William Sharpe, & Jethro Jackson. Issued.

Ordered, that the sum of ninety eight dollars forty seven Cents be appropriated to the use of Reuben Wray, in full for the quota of Hancock County for building a bridge across Buffalo creek at the County line, to be paid when all prior Orders are satisfied.

paid $28 the 30th Sepr 1801. p^d $7.50 4th Feby 1802. p^d 62.97 5th Feb^y.

Monday the 1st June 1801 [27]

Ordered, That the sum of forty five dollars fifty Cents be paid Hamlin Lewis, Esqr, for the use of Henry Jones, to be paid in full for building the bridge over Ogechee at Stith's Mill. Paid.

Ordered, That the sum of eighty seven dollars fifty cents be paid Hamlin Lewis, Esqr, for the use of Henry Jones, to be in full of the quota of this County for building a bridge over Ogechee River at Halliday's Mill. Paid.

Ordered, That the sum of forty nine Dollars twelve and an half Cents be appropriated and paid to John Freeman, in full for the Jail Fees &c of Nathan Tate & William Musgrove & for repairs done on the public Jail of this County.

   5.00 p^d
   3.75 p^d
   9.56¼
  20.37½
  38.68¾

Monday the 1st June 1801 [28]

Ordered, That John Freeman, ~~Henry Moss~~, be appointed first Inspector, Henry Moss Second Inspector, & Thomas Gordon third Inspector of Tob^o at Clement's Warehouse in Sparta, and that John & James Saunders be Pickers & Coopers at said Warehouse, ~~and David Pinkston Cooper~~. Forwarded.

Ordered, That Joel McClendon be & he is hereby appointed first Inspector, John Miles Second Inspector, & John Dysart third Inspector of Tobacco at the Warehouse at Montpellier, Samuel McGehee & Cornelius Whittington Pickers, & Samuel Slaughter Cooper, at said Warehouse. Forwarded.

Ordered, That a tax equal to one fifth part of the General tax be levied for County purposes for the present year, one thousand eight hundred & one.

Monday the 1st June 1801 [29]

Ordered, That Joseph Cooper, jun^r be and he is hereby appointed a Justice of the peace for Capt Barron's District, in place of Myles Greene, Esqr, resigned.

Joseph Turner a Justice of the peace for Capt Chambers's District, in place of William Dent, Esqr, who resides in Capt Tucker's new Dis^t, and Sampson Duggar a Justice of the peace in Capt Lucas's District, in place of Frederick Tucker, Esquire, who (by a division of of Comp^y Dix^s) resides in Capt Tucker's new District.

Forwarded.

Ordered, That the sum of six dollars be appropriated and paid to Philip Turner, in full for work done on the Jail of this County. paid

Ordered, that the sum of six dollars be appropriated and

and paid to Leonard Abercrombie, in full for writing and forwarding [30] County Orders. paid.

Ordered, That a road be laid out the nearest and best way from the Warehouse at Montpellier to the Cedar Shoals by Trice's Mill, that John Trice, John Booth, Senr, & John Dysart be appointed Commissioners, & Isaiah Eiland Overseer of said road from the Warehouse to Trice's Mill, & Theodocius Turk, John Cook, Esqr, & John Gholson Commissioners & Thomas Stephens Overseer of said road from Trice's Mill to Cedar Shoals. Issued.

Ordered, That Edmund Butler, Henry Peak, & Randolph Rutland be and they are hereby appointed Commissioners to view & lay out a road the nearest and best way from Thelford's mill on Ogechee to Sherwood Womack's, thence to the Methodist Meeting house on Powel's creek, thence the nearest and best direction into the road

road leading from Greensborough to Sparta, and that the following [31] hands work thereon, viz. from Thelford's Mill to the Methodist Meeting house.

Freeman Allen, William Thelford, James Simmons, Henry Peek, John Heister, James Alford, John Rogers, James Laurence, Isaac Brewer, Philip Boroughs, Mancil Womack, Elijah Stephens, Saml Pogue, Peter Coffee, Ben^j Whitfield, Ajonadab Reid, Saml Hart, Thos Veazey, Nancy Redding, John Jones, Zebulon

Veazey, Jesse Battle, Ge° West, Michael Dickson, William Lancaster, Thos Lancaster, Needham Jernigan, & John Henderson, Sherwood Womack Overseer.

That the following hands work on the road from the Methodist Meeting house to the road from Greenesboro to Sparta, viz.

Edm^d Butler, Senr, Henry Jernigan, Randolph Rutland, John Michael, Fred^k Tucker, Th° Cooper, James Harvey, Henry Graybill, William Clark, Ja^s Crowder, Jesse Connel, Jeremiah Thompson, Jn° Harvey, Th° Lucas, Philip Allen, Joseph Barksdale, James Randolph, Henry Byrom, James Byrom, Henry Garrett, Robert Simms, John Pope, Henry Long, Richard Runnels, William Johnson, R. B. Fletcher, Milly Roan, Elijah George, Edmond Butler, jun^r, Overseer.

Issued.

Ordered, That Mark Jackson be and he is hereby ~~appointed~~ [32] Continue Overseer of the road leading from John Lamar's to Sparta, and that the hands who formerly worked under [blot] said Jackson continue to work under [blot] him, and that their names be erased off William Hudson's list.

And^w Baxter
A. Comer
Joel McClendon
J. Bailey

Court adjourned until the first Monday in January next.

Attest. Mar Martin, Clk

Monday the 4th January 1802   [33]

Court met pursuant to adjourned.

Present, their Honors   Anderson Comer }
                                             Joel McClendon }
                                             John Wm Devereux } Esquires
                                             Brice Gaither & }
                                             John Coulter }

The Court and Justices of the peace attending, proceeded to the election of a Receiver of tax returns & Collector of taxes for the present year, & the ballots being severally taken & examined for the said Offices, it appeared that Samuel Dent, Esqr was duly elected Receiver of Tax returns & Leonard Abercrombie, Esqr Collector of taxes.

The Court then proceeded to the appointment of Justices of the peace in Capt Humphries's new district, and to fill vacancies which have taken place in the old Company districts by resignation &c of the former Magistrates.

Monday 4th January 1802   [34]

and thereupon,

Ordered, James Scarlett and Lazarus Battle, esquires be and they are hereby appointed Justices of the peace for Capt Humphries's new District.

Walter Hamilton, esquire, a Justice of the peace in Capt Clark's district, in place of John Coulter, Esqr, appointed a Justice of the Inferior Court.

Archibald McLellan Devereux, Esquire a Justice of the peace in Capt Reid's district, in place of John William Devereux, esquire, appointed a Justice of the Inferior Court, and

Jesse Talbert, esq^r a Justice of the peace for Capt Taliaferro's (late Capt Yarborough's) district, in place of Ephraim Moore, Esqr, deceased.

Forwarded.

Ordered, that John Brown be & he is hereby appointed Constable in Capt Barksdale's district, as an assistant to the former Constable.

Matthew Jones a Constable in Capt Lucas's Dis^t

Monday the 4th January 1802   [35]

Edmund Butler a Constable in Capt Tucker's District, Lewis Bandy a Constable in Capt Bullock's District, and that the Constables appointed last year for the other Districts be respectively continued in their several appointments.

Ordered, that the sum of one hundred and thirty nine dollars & fifty cents be appropriated and paid to John Bivins, in full for building a bridge across Town Creek at Bivins's Mill.

[faint]
[faint]
 56¼ p^d
 37½
6.56¼ p^d Paid in full.

Ordered, that the sum of two hundred thirty four dollars and fifty cents be appropriated and paid to John Freeman, Jailer of this County, in full for dieting &c of James Shorter & Nathan Tait, and for a guard on the Jail of four men for fifteen days, during the confinement of the said Nathan Tait.

It appearing to the Court, that the common Jail of this County is out of repair and that the Sheriff has

Monday the 4th January 1802   [36]

has protested against it.

Ordered, that Charles Abercrombie, Esqr, David Clements, & the Sheriff do lett to the lowest bidder the repairing the said Jail in a Strong, secure manner, also the necessary repairs & additions to the bar of the Court house, and providing steps for the doors, and that the Clerk do pay the amount of such contract out of the County funds which may remain in his hands.

         A. Comer
         John Coulter
         Brice Gaither
         Joel McClendon

Court adjourned till the first Saturday in next month.

Attest. Mar Martin, Clk

Saturday the 6th February 1802 [37]

Court met pursuant to adjournment.

Present, their Honors   Anderson Comer }
                             John Coulter   }
                             Brice Gaither & } Esquires
                             John W. Devereux }

Ordered, That Noah Dodridge be and he is hereby appointed Overseer of the road leding from the County line of Greene to Baxter's Mill, Harris Brantley Overseer of the road from Baxter's Mill to the Stoney ridge near Sparta, & James Hall Overseer of the road from Stoney ridge to the old County line.

Forwarded.

Ordered, that Hugh Horton be and he is hereby appointed Overseer of the road leading from his house to the Cedar Shoals.

Saturday the 6th February 1802 [38]

Ordered, That James Ross be and he is hereby appointed Overseer of the road composing the 11th District, viz. from Logdam to Fort creek.

Ordered, That Edmund Butler, John Humphries, & Co^l Thomas Lamar be appointed commissioners to view & lay out a road to lead the nearest and best way from near the mouth of Shoulderbone creek by Richard Hamlin's, to John Humphries's Store, thence into the Montpellier road above Arthur Danielly's.

Ordered, That James Thomas, James Wood, & John Brown be & they are hereby appointed Commissioners to lay out and open a road from where Moses Harris formerly lived at the cross roads to lead into the Saundersville road below Saml Shi's plantation, passing between his two fields where the old road formerly led.

Saturday the 6th February 1802 [39]

Ordered, That Samuel Parker be & he is hereby appointed Overseer of the road leading from Montpellier to the district line on Town creek.

Ordered, That the sum of twenty five Dollars be appropriated & paid to Mrs Henriken, in full for the maintenance & funeral expences of Mary Stein.

23

Ordered, That the sum of thirty Dollars be appropriated and paid for the use of Mary Gasper, a Parishioner, in full for one year's subsistence.

         A. Comer
         Jn° Wm Devereux
         John Coulter
         Brice Gaither

Court adjourned till the last Saturday in this month.

Attest. Mar Martin, Clk

    Saturday the 26th February 1802   [40]

Court met pursuant to adjournment.

Present, their Honors   Anderson Comer }
              John Coulter & } Esquires
              John W. Devereux }

Ordered, That Clement Mullins, George Williams, & Brice Miller be and they are hereby appointed Commissioners to lay out a road from Mullins's Mill on the Oconee to the road leading from the Cedar Shoals to Sparta at Joseph Carr's plantation, and William Mathews Overseer of said road.

Ordered, That John Hamilton, Archibald M. Devereux, & James Scarlett, Esquires be and they are hereby appointed Commissioners to lay out a road the nearest and best way from the corner of lot

    Saturday the 26th February 1802   [41]

lot N° 17 on Broad & Rabun Streets in Sparta, to Devereux's Mill on Buffalo, & from thence to the road leading from Mossey's to Montpellier, so as to join said road on the North side of James Scarlett's plantation, that John Middlebrooks be Overseer of said road from Scarlett's to Musselwhite's plantation, & Philip Levar Overseer from Musselwhite's to where said road starts on Broad Street in Sparta. issued.

Ordered, that the sum of sixteen dollars thirty six & an half Cents be allowed Leonard Abercrombie, esquire, being the County tax on insolvents, agreeably to a recommendation of the Grand Jury, and the further sum of * seventeen dollars eighty six Cents, being an allowance of 5 P Cent for collecting the County tax of the year 1800.

16.36½
* 17.86

Ordered, That the sum of two dollars be appropriated and paid to Hamlin Lewis. esquire, in full of his fees against James Bradley, lately tried for horse stealing in the Superior Court of this County.

Saturday the 26th February 1802 [42]

Ordered, That the sum of nineteen dollars twenty five Cents be appropriated & paid to John Freeman, in full for the Jail fees of James Bradley.

Ordered, That Tavern license be granted to James Scarlett & Thomas Norton, to keep a house of entertainment at their Store, and also to Joachim Dudley Swinney, at his residence in this County, and that the Clerk do take bonds with good securities of said Scarlett & Swinney in terms of the Act.

Ordered, That John Maclemore be & he is hereby appointed a Constable for Capt Humphries's new District.

Anderson Comer
John Coulter
Jn° Wm Devereux

Saturday the 26th February 1802 [43]

Ordered, That William Saunders & John Lamar, esquires be and they are hereby appointed Overseers of the poor for this County.

Anderson Comer
John Coulter
Jn° Wm Devereux

Court adjourned until the last Friday in Ap^l next.

Attest. Mar Martin, Clk

Friday the 30th April 1802

Court met pursuant to adjournment.

Present, their Honors   Anderson Comer }
                                   John Coulter & } Esquires
                                   Brice Gaither   }

Friday the 30th April 1802   [44]

Ordered, That James Harvey, esquire be & he is hereby appointed Overseer of the road leading from Zachariah Middleton's to Powelton, as far as Henry Graybill's plantation.

Ordered, That John Smith be and he is hereby appointed Overseer of the road from the mouth of Shoulderbone, to where it intersects the road leading from John Lamar's to John Rivers's, Hubbard Brown Overseer of the S^d road leading from where it intersects Lamar's road, to the Cedar Shoals (from Sparta) below John Barron's, and John Humphries Overseer from thence to the Montpellier road, agreeably to the report of Thomas Lamar, John Humphries, and Edmund Butler, esquires.

Friday the 30th April 1802   [45]

Ordered, That the sum of eight dollars be appropriated and paid to Thomas Carroll, in full for making steps to the doors of the Court house. paid.

Ordered, that Barnaby Shivers, esquires be and he is hereby appointed a Justice of the Peace for Capt Barksdale's district, in place of James Garey, esq^r, resigned.

Ordered, That Tavern license be granted to Jesse Sanford, esq^r, to continue one year.

Ordered, That Tavern license be granted to Willie Abercrombie for twelve months.

Ordered, That the following hands do work on

Friday the 30th April 1802   [46]

on the road from Harrison's cross roads to Saml Shi's plantation, viz.

Isaac Hill, Isaac Hill, jun^r, John Norsworthy, Allen Bird, Dempsey Hughes, [blank] Moore, Joel Pound, Levi Lary, Frederick Tilman, Richard A. Blount, Micajah Pickard, John Dawson, Solomon Phillips, & Jesse Page Overseer. issued.

Ordered, That Jonathan Day be & he is hereby appointed Overseer of the road from Big Island Creek to the road near Arthur Danielly's. issued.

Ordered, That Laban Turk be and he is hereby appointed Overseer of the road leading from the Cedar Shoals to Borland's mill. Issued.

        Anderson Comer
        John Coulter
        Brice Gaither

Court adjourned until the 1st Monday in June next.

Attest. Mar Martin, Clk

      Monday the 7th June 1802   [47]

Court met pursuant to adjournment.

Present, their Honors   Anderson Comer }
              John Coulter   } Esq^{rs}
              Joel McClendon & }
              John W. Devereux }

Ordered, That John Freeman be and he is hereby appointed 1st Inspector, Henry Moss 2nd, & Eppes Moss 3rd Inspector of Tobacco at the Sparta Warehouse. Forwarded.

Ordered, That John Miles, Esqr be and he is hereby appointed 1st, Jeremiah Walker 2nd, & William Miles 3rd Inspector of Tobacco at Montpellier Warehouse. Forwarded.

Ordered, That the sum of sixty four dollars

Monday the 7th June 1802 [48]

and fifty cents be appropriated and paid to John Buckner, as a balance due him for painting the Courthouse, agreeably to a report of the Commissioners of the 12th May last. Paid in full.

Ordered, That Moses Wiley, esquire be and he is hereby appointed Justice of the peace for Capt Cato's District, in place of Jonathan Adams, Esqr, resigned. & Richard Morgan, Esqr a Justice of the Peace for Capt Dixon's District, in place of Robert Tate, Esqr, resigned. Forwarded.

Ordered, That the sum of twelve dollars be appropriated and paid to Robert Buchannan, for damages sustained by him in laying out a public road through his plantation. relinquished.

Ordered, That the sum of six dollars be appropriated and paid to Joseph Paramour, for damages adjudged him, for laying out a public road thro his plantation. relinquished.

Monday the 7th June 1802 [49]

Ordered, That the following Tavern rates be taken for the present year, and no more, viz.

	Cents
For a Dinner with fresh meat	25
" Breakfast	18¾
" Fodder sufficient for a Horse per night	12½
" Corn or Oats Pr Gallon	12½
" Lodging P^r night	6¼
" Jamaica Spirits per half pint	18¾
" Holland Gin P^r ditto	18¾
" Northward D^o & Whiskey p^r ditto	12½
" West India Rum p^r ditto	18¾
" Northward or Continental Rum per Ditto	12½
" Apple or Peach Brandy good Quality	12½

Ordered, That Henry Moss and Jecamiah Moore be and they are hereby appointed Overseers of the poor, in addition to those already appointed.

Monday the 7th June 1802 [50]

Ordered, That the following hands do work on the road from Montpellier Warehouse to Derris's Creek, viz.

Isaac Jackson, Thos Tolar, Danl Candler, James Courson, Farish Carter, Thomas Graham, John Candler, Wm Bruce, Samuel McGehee, Jeremiah Walker, Philip Cook, John Leith, Moses Dysart, Mrs Robertson, Abraham Miles, Danl Candler Slaughter, Marvel McClendon, Mrs Beard, James Hogg, John B. Devereux, Tilman Buckner, Leven S. McClendon, John Marcus, John Dysart, Lewis May, Mr Irwin, Mr Martin, & David Hubert Overseer, Isaiah Eiland, Thomas Miles, Benjamin Catching, Philip Catching, Obadiah Morris, Elisha Moran, John Murphey, William Bivin, Cadwall Raines, Fras Beard, William Freeman, Jesse Talbert, W. Buckles, Abraham Miles, William Rhodes, Jeremiah Miles, and David Hubert, Overseer. Issued.

Monday the 7th June 1802 [51]

Ordered, That the following hands work on the road leading from Joel McClendon's, Esqr to the Washington County line, viz.

James Thweatt's hands, Benjamin T[torn], Cornelius Whittington's hands, Ephraim Whitting[torn], Richard Whittington, John Whittington, James Whittington, Aaron Whittington, Jeratt Whittington, Samuel Slaughter, John Brown, John Miles, and Joseph Porter, Overseer. issued.

Ordered, That the following hands work on the road leading from Montpellier Warehouse to William Bivins', viz.

William Bivins, Jonathan Colbert, John Williamson, Thomas Hawkins, Jacob Speckard, Jacob Bosworth, Archelaus Ferrell, Belah Cook, Thomas Cavenah, Mrs Cathell, Edards Brown, Wm Brown, William Miles, Wilson Mercer, John Connor, Dempsey Justice, Greene Lea, Elijah Greenlea, Jos Miles, George Simpson, James Montgomery, David Montgomery, John Montgomery, Michael Rogers, Thomas

Monday the 7th June 1802 [52]

Thomas Hadway, William Miles, George Cavenah, Alexander Greene, Robt Hill, Samuel Kirkpatrick, Ransom Lea, & Samuel Parker, Overseer. issued.

Ordered, That Tavern license be granted to Joel McClendon, to keep a house of entertainment at Montpellier.

Ordered, That Tavern license be granted Abraham & James Miles, to keep a house of entertainment at their residence near Montpellier. Paid 9.56.

Ordered, That a tax equal to one fifth part of the General tax, for the present year one thousand eight hundred and two, be levied and collected for County purposes.

Ordered, That license be granted to John Comer & Leonard Abercrombie, to keep a Tavern or house of entertainment at their Store at Rural Mount.

Monday the 7th June 1802 [53]

Ordered, That James Garey, esquire be and he is hereby appointed a Justice of the Peace in Capt Bonner's District, in place of James Mitchell, esq^r, resigned. Forwarded.

Ordered, That John Lucas & Archibald M. Devereux, esquires do convene with the Sheriff, to lett the repairing of the public Jail, in a strong manner, to the lowest bidder & take bond of the undertaker for the faithful performance of his duty.

Ordered, That the sum of eighty Seven and an half Cents be appropriated and paid to Willie Abercrombie, in full for a padlock furnished for the public Jail of this County. to be p^d to H. Lewis.

Ordered, That the following hands do work on the road leading from the corner of lot N° 17

Monday the 7th June 1802 [54]

in Sparta to Devereux's Mill, viz.

Charles Abercrombie, John Hamilton's hands, James Thweatt's hands, William Reese, Henry Mitchell, John Lucas's hands, Duke Hamilton, Henry Thornton, James Musselwhite, John Stell, Robert Stell, Richard Bonner, & Philip Levar, Overseer. Issued. &

The following hands to work on the road from Musselwhite's to Scarlett's Store, viz.

Jacob Dennis, John Dennis, Thomas Vickers, James Boswell, John Stanton, Lindsay Roberts, David McAllister, Samuel Devereux, Benjamin Bolt, [blank] Russel, [blank] Collins, Thomas Norton, Cader Powell, & John Middlebrooks, Overseer. Issued.

Anderson Comer
John Coulter
Joel McClendon
Jn° Wm Devereux

Court adjourned until the last Saturday in October next.

Attest. Mar Martin, Clk

Saturday the 30th October 1802   [55]

Court met pursuant to adjournment.

Present, their Honors   Anderson Comer }
     John Coulter & } Esquires
     John W. Devereux }

Ordered, That James Comer, Thomas Stephens, & Francis Lawson, esquires be and they are hereby appointed Commissioners to view & lay off a road the nearest & best way from the ford on the Oconee river near Fra^s Harrison's to William Hutchinson's, thence to George Stephens's, thence by Comer's & Abercrombie's Store, & thence a direct course, so as to interest the road from John Lamar's to Sparta, near Mrs Jackson's plantation, and that George Stephens be Overseer of that road.

Ordered, That Andrew Borland, Jesse Sanford, and

Saturday the 30th October 1802   [56]

and Robert McGinty, esquires be and they are hereby appointed Commissioners to view a road to lead between the plantation of James Thomas and the plantations of Abner Abercrombie & John Booth, jun^r, to begin where the road leading from the ford on Big Island creek to Arthur Danielly's passes by the corner of said Abercrombie's plantation, and to join said road from Island creek at the South end of James Thomas's lane, and make report to the next Inferior Court for the County of Hancock of the convenience & propriety of said road.

> John Coulter
> Anderson Comer
> Jn° Wm Devereux

Court adjourned until the first Monday in January next.

Attest. Mar Martin, Clk

Monday the 3rd January 1803 [57]

This being the day of meeting pursuant to adjournment.

Their Honors John Coulter and Brice Gaither attended, and William Rabun, esquire, having been appointed in place of Joel McClendon, esq^r, resigned, attended and being qualified agreeably to Law, took his seat.

The Court proceeded to the appointment of Constables for the several Company Districts in this County, & thereupon

Ordered, That John Brown be and he is hereby appointed Constable for Capt Barksdale's Dis^t.

George Williams for Capt Williams' District.

James Terry additional Constable for Capt Reed's Dis^t.

William Miles Const^l for Capt Taliaferro's Dis^t.

Saml Pope additional Constable for Capt Strother's Dis^t.

Solomon Barfield, Junr for Capt Latimore's District.

and that all Constables now in Office do continue in the exercise of their duties for the term of one year.

Monday the 3rd January 1803 [58]

Ordered, That license be granted to William Bivins and Matthew Kinchen, to keep houses of entertainment at their residences in this County for one year from this date.

The Court & the Justices of the peace present proceeded to the election of a Receiver of Tax returns and collector of Taxes, and on closing the polls and counting out the ballots, it appeared that John Comer was duly elected as Receiver of Tax returns and Leonard Abercrombie Collector of Taxes for the present year.

        Brice Gaither
        Wm Rabun
        John Coulter

Court adjourned until the Second Friday in this month.

Attest. Mar Martin, Clk

Friday the 14th January 1803 [59]

Court met pursuant to adjournment.

Present, their Honors   John Coulter }
            Brice Gaither } Esquires
            John W. Devereux }
            William Rabun }

Ordered, That John Freeman be and he is hereby appointed Overseer of the road leading from Sparta to the Piney woods house, to George Cowin's, in place of George Cowin, resigned.

Ordered, that the following hands work upon the road from George Cowin's to the Piney woods house, viz.

Enias Mershon, John Vinson, Joseph Knowles, Larkin Turner, William Hearne, Elisha Vinson, Edward Flowers, Thomas Shockley, Neubal Waller, Lewis Bandy, Abraham Betts, James Carter, David Carter, Thomas Turner, William Turner, Thos Williams, & Manning Bowling, Overseer. Issued.

Friday the 14th January 1803 [60]

Ordered, That Lewis Barnes be and he is hereby appointed Overseer of the road from Parham's Mill to the Sparta road, in place of Abner Lockett, removed. Issued.

Ordered, that William Griggs be and he is hereby appointed Overseer of the road from Fort creek near Nathan Saunders' to the Montpellier road, in place of Philip Pritchett, resigned. Issued.

Ordered, that the following hands do work on the road from Nathaniel Waller's lane to the Greenesborough road near Sparta, viz.

Edward Bazer, John Stanton, William Stanton, Francis Jeter, Nathaniel Waller, William Bazer, John McLemore, Duke Hamilton, John Hamilton, jun^r, William

Friday the 14th Jany 1803 [61]

William Sallard, Job Tison, Epps Brown, John Crowder, Henry Mitchell, Frederick Equals, John C. Peak, & Bird Ferrell, Overseer. Issued.

Ordered, That Benjamin Whitfield, Randolph Rutland, & Thomas Cooper, Esquires be and they are hereby appointed Commissioners to view & lay out a road from Mrs Nancy Reddin's to John Rudisell's mill, and from thence to the Sparta road near Joseph Cooper's plantation. Issued.

Ordered, That the following hands work on & keep in repair the road from James Musselwhite's to the road leading from Sparta to Mrs Hunter's, viz.

William Reese, John Lucas, Philip Levar, Richard Bonner, Henry Thornton, James Langford, James Musselwhite, Lindsay Roberts, Danl Johnson, Robert Stell, Drury Musselwhite, and John Hamilton, Overseer. Issued.

Friday the 14th January 1803 [62]

Ordered, That the sum of twenty three Dollars eighty Seven and an half cents be appropriated and paid to Doctor Timothy W. Rossiter, in full for his attendance on & medicine administered to William Runnels, an infirm person. ~~Issued~~.

Ordered, That the sum of sixteen Dollars and fifty cents be appropriated and paid to Thomas Carroll, in full for repairs &c done to the public Jail of this County. ~~Issued.~~

Ordered, That Joseph Henry be and he is hereby appointed Overseer of the road from Jesse Connell's to the forks of the road at Powelton, in place of Jesse Connell, resigned. ~~Issued.~~

Ordered, That Edmund Corley be and he is hereby appointed Overseer of the road from the forks thereof at Powelton to Lucas's Mill and that the following hands do work thereon. Issued.

Friday the 14th January 1803   [63]

Ebenezer Doughty, Peter Wright, John Simmons, Robert Greene, William Lee, Septimus Weatherby, Sampson Duggar, John Burch, William Lord, Michael Harvey, Senr, James Lucas, & Betsy Lucas' hands. Issued.

Ordered, That Thomas Clarke be and he is hereby appointed Overseer of the road leading from Powelton to the Sunbury road below Saml Shi's plantation, as far as from Powelton to Mitchell's road, and the following hands to work thereon, viz.

Greene Lea, James Tomlin, Joseph Minton, Joseph Grant, & Levi Speight. Issued

Willis Shivers, Overseer from Mitchell's road to Fulsom's creek, and the following hands to work thereon, viz.

John Kilgore, Charles Kilgore, David Dickson, Matthew Rabun, William Rabun, William Speight, William Hardwick, Jonas Shivers, & William Battle. Issued.

Friday the 14th January 1803   [64]

Mark Gonder Overseer from Fulsom's creek to the George Town road, and the following hands to work thereon, viz.

Samuel Pope, James Wilson, Benjamin Cook, James Tilman, William Andrews, Thomas Mason, John Kelley, William Seale, Isaac Hill, Senr, & William Murphey. Issued.

Allen Bird, from the George Town road to the Sunbury road, and the following hands to work thereon, viz.

Elizabeth Merrit, John Pound, Frederick Tilman, James Wood, Solomon Phillips, Jesse Page, Alex^r Herring, & Arthur Herring. & that John Brown be & he is hereby appointed a Commissioner of said road, in place of James Thomas, removed. Issued.

Ordered, That Littleton Reese be and

Friday the 14th January 1803 [65]

and he is hereby appointed Overseer of the road from George Cowin's to Obadiah Richardson's Store. Issued.

Ordered, That the following hands do work on the road from the Piney woods house to George Town, as far as to Barksdale's old Machine on the Sparta road, viz.

William Mangham, Samuel Lewis, William Driskill, John Driskill, Isaac Carter, Aaron Strother, George Strother, Richard Strother, David Strother, Charles Buckner, Philip Jackson, Joel Moody, Isaac Elliot, Jesse Allen, Robert Allen, James Allen, & William Mangham, Overseer. Issued.

Ordered, That the following hands do work on the road from Powelton to Burch's Mill on Ogechee, viz.

James Harvey, jun^r, [blank] Ingram, Daniel Blankenship, William Northern, Sion West,

Friday the 14th January 1803 [66]

Nicholas Darby, William Lee, Ben^j Buchannan, Francis Smith, Matthew Jones, & Frier Robertson, Overseer. Issued.

Ordered, That Lewis Moss be and he is hereby appointed a Justice of the peace in Capt Strother's District, in place of William Rabun, esq^r, resigned.

Tisey Thomas a Justice of the peace in Capt Dixon's Dis^t, in place of Richard Morgan, who declined accepting that appointment, and

William Lee a Justice of the peace for Capt ~~Lucas~~' Johnson's Dis^t, in place of John Veazey, esq^r, resigned. Forwarded.

William Bullock a Justice of the peace in Capt Bullock's Dis^t, in place of Joseph B. Chambers, esquire, removed, and

Hubert Reynolds a Justice of

Friday the 14th January 1803 [67]

of the peace in Capt Gray's Dis^t, in place of Robert McGinty, esquire, resigned.

Ordered, That that part of the road contemplated by an order of the 26th February last, which extends from the corner of lot N° 17 on Broad Street to where it would interest the road to Mrs Hunter's, be and the same is discontinued.

         Wm Rabun
         John Coulter
         Brice Gaither
         Jno Wm Devereux

Court adjourned until the first Friday in April next.

Attest. Mar Martin, Clk

Friday the 1st April 1803 [68]

Court met pursuant to adjournment.

Present, their Honors   John Coulter }
            Brice Gaither & } Esquires
            William Rabun &}
            Thompson Bird }

Ordered, That Edmund Oneal be and he is hereby appointed Overseer of the road leading from Baxter's Mill to the Creek at Major Trippe's old plantation, in place of Reuben Hearndon, resigned, and that the following hands to work thereon, viz.

Reuben Hearndon, David Henry, Absalom Harris, Samuel Harris, William Hunt, Judkins Hunt, James Hunt, Turner Hunt, Samuel White, John White, Henry Turner, Polly Brewer, John McKay, Joseph Johnson, Abner Reid, Stephen Daniell, Thomas Rivers, & Francis Ross.

Friday the 1st April 1803 [69]

Ordered, That the Road leading from John Humphris's to Montpellier, through the lands of Robert Buchannan and Joseph Paramour, on the lower fork of Rocky creek, be turned (agreeably to the demarkation of John Harbirt, Joseph Howard, and Joel King) so as to leave said Buchannan's old Plantation and paramor's to the right hand as the road leads to Montpellier, the said Buchannan and Paramour opening said road agreeably to law and relinquishing all damages assessed for their favor by a Jury, on account of the old road running thro' their plantations.

Ordered, That Isaac Newsom have leave to turn and put in repair the public road leading thro' his plantation, so as to begin at the old road near his gate, and to run by his house into the old road near a pond, leaving the pond to the left hand.

Friday the 1st April 1803 [70]

Ordered, That the sum of fifty four dollars be appropriated and paid to John Peace, as full compensation for the maintenance of William Clark, a parishioner for the year 1802. Paid as p^r Rec^t.

Ordered, That Samuel Ewing be and he is hereby appointed Overseer of the road comprising the 18th District, leading from Sparta to Stith's Mill, as far as Barksdale's fork, in place of James Huddleston, resigned, and that the following hands do work thereon, viz.

Jesse Veazey, Thomas Gordon, James Evans, John Buckner, junr, Jeffery Barksdale, Joel Buckner, John Buckner, Senr, Thomas Gay, Willie Buckner, Alexander Torry, Joseph Reese, James McNeill. Purnel Trader, [blank] Maddux, Howell A. Reese, Kennon B. Heath, James Huddleston, Barnaby Shivers, and Thomas Ewing. Issued.

Friday the 1st April 1803 [71]

Ordered, that Tavern license be granted to Elijah Lingo and William Brown, to keep houses of entertainment at their several places of residence, for twelve months.

Ordered, That Allen Pope be and he is hereby appointed Overseer of the road leading from the Piney woods house to Stith's Mill, as far as the branch below Spikes's plantation, and that the following hands work thereon, viz.

Joseph Maddux, Thomas Grace, Benjamin Evans, Abner Atkinson, Mary Lockhart, Jesse Pope, & Henry Pope, Robert Gilmore, & Thomas Worsham. Issued.

Ordered, That the sum of twenty dollars be appropriated and paid to Samuel Hall (Coroner) for summoning & holding an Inquest on the boddy of Reddick Grier, and the child of Patsy Sturdivant.

Ordered, That Peter Hutchinson

Friday the 1st April 1803 [72]

be and he is hereby appointed a Commissioner, in conjunction with James Comer and Thomas Stephens (in place of Francis Lawson, Esqr, dec^d) to view and lay out a road the nearest and best way from the foard on the Oconee near Francis Lawson's plantation, to William Hutchinson's, & thence agreeably to an order of the 30th October last.

          Brice Gaither
          Wm Rabun
          John Coulter
          Thompson Bird

The Court adjourned until Court in Course.

Attest. Mar Martin, Clk

Monday the 6th June 1803 [73]

Court met pursuant to adjournment.

Present, their Honors   John Coulter }
                John W. Devereux } Esquires
                William Rabun }
                Brice Gaither }

Ordered, That Tavern license be issued to Robert Lenoir, Eli Harris, Howell Anderson Reese, & Philip Turner, to keep houses of entertainment at their places of residence.

Ordered, That Josiah Dennis be & he is hereby appointed Constable in & for Capt Humphries' District.

Ordered, That one Copy of Marbury & Crawford's Digest of the Laws of this State be furnished by the Clerk of the Inferior Court to the Justices of

Monday the 6th June 1803 [74]

the Inferior Court severally, to the Sheriff, to the Clerks of the Superior and Court of Ordinary, and one to the use of each Justice of the Company Districts in the County, they severally signing a receipt in the following words, viz.

"Received this [blank] day of [blank] 1803, of Martin Martin, Clerk of the Inferior Court of Hancock County, one Copy of Marbury & Crawford's Digest of the Laws of this State, to be returned to the said Court when the Office which I now hold shall become vacant."

Ordered, That Benjamin J. Harper be and he is hereby appointed Overseer of the road leading from Fort Creek to Logdam, comprising the 11th District, in place of James Ross, resigned, & that the same hands do work under him as are included in the list for said District. Issued.

Monday the 6th June 1803 [75]

Ordered, That Dudley Hargrove be and he is hereby appointed Overseer of the road from Baxter's Mill to the Stoney ridge near Sparta, in place of Harris Brantley, resigned, and that the following hands work thereon, viz.

Edmund Abercrombie, John Gay, Richard Respess, Isham Reese, John Grammer, Henry Brown, Edmund Taylor, George Runnels, Levin Turner, Samuel Turner, Zadok Stinson, Thomas Brantley, Alexander Reid, James Saunders, Mrs Frances Shackelford, William Harper, John Reid, John Brodnax, John Turner, John Trippe, William Trippe, Bolling Hall, James Reese, James Greene, Joshua Haynes, John Brown, Frederick Ray, Charles Hurt, Elijah Palmer, James McCaughey, Thomas Huff, Shadrach Roe, James Reid, Nicholas Booty, Andrew Baxter, Elisha Harris, Eli Harris, John Chandler, Elisha Self, & M^{rs} [blank] Trippe, & Harris Brantley. Issued.

Ordered, That John Brown have liberty to turn the road leading through his lane from Sparta to Baxter's Mill, so as to leave the old road

Monday the 6th June 1803 [76]

between his and John Gay's plantation to pass through his, Brown's, plantation North of the old road by said Brown's house, & to join the old road above his plantation.

Ordered, That the road laid out by Joseph Henry, beginning at the end of Burch's lane and crossing the Creek below the old Ford, so as to run through a lane between Needham Jernigan's & Henry's plantations, be established as a public road, and that the old road be discontinued, and that the following hands do work thereon, viz.

James Throgmorton, Jesse Connell, Joseph Cooper, Hardy Jernigan, David Long, John Henry, Benjamin Henry, Charles Goss, John Colbert, Nancy Stewart's hands, James Jernigan, & Joseph Henry, Overseer. Issued.

Monday the 6th June 1803 [77]

Ordered, That Alexander Greene, Joel McClendon, and Jacob Buckles be and they are hereby appointed Commissioners to view and lay out a road the nearest and best way from Miles's Store to Holt's Mills on Town Creek, and that the following hands work thereon, viz.

Alexander Greene, overseer, James Cathell, Jesse Talbert, Esqr, David Montgomery, and Jacob Buckles. Issued.

Ordered, That Seymore Catching be & he is hereby appointed Overseer of the road from Devereux Creek to Rocky Creek, & Hugh Moss Comer Overseer of said road from Rocky Creek to the Cedar Shoals on the Oconee. Issued.

Ordered, That Sampson Duggar & Edmund Corley, esquires be and they are hereby appointed Commissioners of the Bridge at Burch's Mill, in place of James Lucas & George Norsworthy, esquires, deceased. Issued.

Monday the 6th June 1803 [78]

Ordered, That Tavern license be granted to Arrenton Purify, to keep entertainment at his place of residence.

Ordered, That Joel Hurt, Senr be and he is hereby exonerated from the payment of a poll tax.

Ordered, That the sum of thirty Dollars be appropriated & paid to the Overseers of the poor, for the sustenance of Thomas Smith, a parishioner for the year 1802. Paid.

Ordered, That the sum of thirty five Dollars sixty two & an half cents be appropriated & paid to John Freeman, in full compensation for Jail fees & receiving and dieting Joseph Bridges & Elisha Rogers, prisoners lately confined in Jail.

Ordered, That the sum of four dollars be appropriated and paid to Hamlin Lewis, Esquire, in

Monday the 6th June 1803 [79]

in full for his fees & Services for committing, taking out for trial, & Hab Corp in the cases of the State against Joseph & James Bridges.

Ordered, That the following sums be appropriated and paid to Hamlin Lewis, Esqr for & in behalf of the persons following, viz.

To Samuel John four Dollars	$4.00
" Starling Savage three Dollars	3.00
" Major Peace four Dollars	4.00
" Kennon Heath one Dollar	1.00
" James H. Jones one Dollar	1.00
" Joseph Reese one Dollar	1.00
" James McNeill one Dollar	1.00
" James Lewis four Dollars	4.00
" Buckner Morris four Dollars	4.00
" John Mitchell three Dollars	3.00
" William Sanford two Dollars	2.00
" Frederick Sanford one Dollar	1.00
" Purnell Trader one Dollar	1.00
" John M. Sherman one Dollar	1.00
" Philip Turner one Dollar	1.00
	32.00

amounting to thirty two dollars as compensation for

Monday the 6th June 1803 [80]

for their services in guarding the Jail, during the confinement of Joseph & James Bridges.

Ordered, That Willie Abercrombie & Archibald M. Devereux, esquires be and they are hereby appointed Commissioners to examine & have the necessary repairs done to the public Jail of this County.

> Wm Rabun
> Jno Wm Devereux
> Brice Gaither
> John Coulter

Court adjourned until the third Monday in August next.

Attest. Mar Martin, Clk

Monday the 15th August 1803 [81]

Court met pursuant to adjournment.

Present, their Honors   John Coulter   }
                         John W. Devereux   } Esquires
                         William Rabun   }

Ordered, That Tavern license be granted to Allen Greene & Co, to keep a house of entertainment at their residence in Montpellier for twelve months from this date.

Rec^d $9.56¼ the 1 Jany 1804.

> Wm Rabun
> Jno Wm Devereux
> John Coulter

Court adjourned till Saturday the 27th of this month.

Attest. Mar Martin, Clk

Saturday the 27th August 1803 [82]

Court met pursuant to adjournment.

Present, their Honors   John Coulter   }
                        Brice Gaither } Esquires
                        William Rabun }

Ordered, That Tavern license be granted to Daniel Osgood, to keep a house of entertainment at his residence in Montpellier.

Ordered, That the Sum of sixty nine dollars eighty Seven & an half cents, in full for the Jail fees and dietting of James Bridges and Elisha Rogers, be appropriated and paid to John Freeman, Jailor of this County.

Ordered, that the sum of two dollars be appropriated & paid to Hamlin Lewis, in full for empannelling Juries in the Cases of the State vs Joseph & Ja^s Bridges.

Saturday the 27th August 1803 [83]

Ordered, That the sum of thirty one dollars forty Seven & an half Cents be and the same is hereby appropriated to James Dubose, being the amount of Sale of an Estray mare tolled by Ann Kenan, after deducting the lawful fees.

Brice Gaither
Wm Rabun
John Coulter

Court adjourned till the 2nd Saturday in ~~this~~ next month.

Attest. Mar Martin, Clk

Saturday the 10th September 1803 [84]

Court met pursuant to adjournment.

Present, their Honors   John Coulter   }
                        Brice Gaither } Esquires
                        William Rabun }

Ordered, That William Cureton, Esquire be and he is hereby appointed a Commissioner on the part of this County, to act with the Commissioners who may be appointed by the Counties of Warren & Washington ~~Counties~~, to let to the lowest bidder the repairing a Bridge across Ogeechee river at George Town.

Ordered, That Tavern license be granted to James Reddock, to keep a house of entertainment at his residence in this County.

Saturday the 10th September 1803 [85]

Ordered, that the following hands do work on the road leading from George Town to Benjamin Averett's, viz.

Thomas Dixon, John Dixon, John Averett, Archelaus Averett, Jeremiah Averett, David Averett, Matthew Averett, John Shoulders, David Shoulders, Edward Shoulders, Burwell Rachels, George Rachels, William Rachels, Thomas Pritchett, Nehemiah Smith, William Trent, Wm Hollyman, Giles Kelley, William Curtis, William Pritchett, & Abraham Smith, Overseer.

Issued by Elijah Warthen.

Ordered, That the sum of twenty three Dollars & twenty five cents be appropriated and paid to Willie Abercrombie, in full for Locks & Blacksmith's & Carpenter's work for the public Jail of this County.

paid $23.25.

Saturday the 10th September 1803 [86]

Ordered, That the sum of three Dollars be appropriated & paid to Frederick Temple, and the sum of four dollars appropriated & paid to Edward H. Currie, to be in full of their charge, the said Temple three & the said Currie four days guarding James & Joseph Bridges.

Ordered, That the sum of three Dollars be appropriated & paid to John Clements, for the use of his Negro Smith, Ben, to be in full for putting on & taking off the Irons, the Irons ordered on Barnes & Bridges.

Ordered, that the sum of Seven Dollars eight & a quarter Cents be appropriated & paid to William Brodnax, in full for making an Estray Pound & furnishing locks & Hinges thereto.

Saturday the 10th September 1803 [87]

Ordered, That the sum of five Dollars be appropriated and paid to Thomas Foster, in full for repairs done to the Bar of the Court house & Jury Boxes.

Ordered, That John Comer, esquire be & he is hereby appointed a Justices of the Peace for Capt Lewis's District, in place of John Ragan, Esqr, resigned, and & that

Nathaniel Waller, esquire be and he is hereby appointed a Justice of the peace for Capt Humphries's District, in place of James Scarlett, esquire, resigned.

Forwarded.

Ordered, That license be granted to Mark Moore, to keep a house of entertainment at his residence in this County.

Saturday the 10th Septr 1803 [88]

Mr James Thomas, having made satisfactory proof to the Court, that two Heifers tolled by John Middlebrooks & sold as Estrays were his right & property.

Ordered, That the sum of seven dollars nineteen & an half cents be appropriated & paid to said James Thomas, being in full for the amount of Sales of the said Estrays, after deducting lawful fees.

Ordered, that a tax equal to one fifth part of the General tax be levied as a County tax for the year 1803.

Ordered, that the sum of one dollar be appropriated & paid to Frederick Sanford, in full for one days attendance as a Guard on Bridges.

Ordered, That Peter Boyle, Jesse Veazey, & James Harvey, Esquires be and they are hereby appointed

Saturday the 10th Septr 1803 [89]

appointed Overseers of the poor, in addition to those heretofore appointed.

John Coulter
Brice Gaither
Wm Rabun

Court adjourned until Court in course.

Attest. Mar Martin, Clk

Monday the 2nd January 1804   [90]

Court met pursuant to adjournment.

Present, their Honors   Brice Gaither }
    John W. Devereux }
    William Rabun } Esquires
    Stephen Evans }
    Thomas Cooper }

Ordered, That license be granted to James H. Jones & C°, to keep a house of entertainment at their residence in Sparta.

Ordered, that license be granted to Mark Gonder, to keep a house of entertainment at his residence in this County. Rec^d $9.56¼.

Ordered, that license be granted to Isaac Hill, to keep a house of entertainment at his residence in this County.

Ordered, that license be granted to Seth Kennedy, to Keep a house of entertainment at his residence in this County.

Monday the 2nd January 1804   [91]

The Court and Justices of the peace attending, proceeded to the election of a receiver of Tax returns and Collector of Taxes for the present year, & on closing the polls, it appeared that John Comer, esquire was duly elected Receiver of tax returns & Leonard Abercrombie, esquire Collector of taxes.

Ordered, That license be granted to James Miles and Thomas Taylor (under the firm of Miles & Taylor) to keep a house of entertainment at their residence in this County. Rec^d $9.56¼.

Ordered, That license be granted to John Davidson, to Keep a house of entertainment at his residence in this County. Rec^d $9.56¼.

Ordered, That license be granted to Thomas & James Crowder, to keep a house of entertainment at their residence in this County.

Monday the 2nd January 1804 [92]

Ordered, That the sum of twenty five dollars per Annum be appropriated and paid to Anderson Comer, esq^r, for the use of Nancy Gann, an infirm child, the daughter of Jenny Gann, to commence with the year one thousand eight hundred, inclusive.

Ordered, That license be granted to Thomas Simmons, to keep a house of entertainment at his residence in this County.

Ordered, That license be granted to Henry Brown & Richard Davenport, to keep a house of entertainment at their residence in this County.

Ordered, That William Chandler, Esqr be and he is hereby appointed a Justice of the Peace for Capt Strother's district, in place of Lewis Moss, esq^r, resigned.

That John Andrews be and he is hereby appointed a Justice of the peace for Capt Latimore's District, in place of William Chandler, Esqr, removed.

Monday the 2nd January 1804 [93]

That William McLellan, Esqr be and he is hereby appointed a Justice of the peace for Capt Slaughter's District, in place of Peter Coffee, esq^r, deceased.

That Singleton Holt, esq^r be and he is hereby appointed a Justice of the peace for Capt Bullock's District, in place of Joseph Turner, esq^r, resigned.

That Samuel M. Devereux, Esqr be and he is hereby appointed a Justice of the peace for Capt Humphries's District, in place of Lazarus Battle, esq^r, resigned.

Forwarded.

Ordered, That the following Constables be and they are hereby appointed for the respective Districts following, viz.

For Capt Humphries's District	Smith Waller
Capt Latimore's District	John Hall
Capt Catoe's District	William Clower

Monday the 2nd January 1804 [94]

For Capt Taliaferro's District   Francis Beard, in addition to
William Miles now acting in S^d District
  Capt Lewis's District   John Rivers & Abraham Womack
  Capt Graybill's District   Nathaniel Halley
  Capt Eiland's District   John McDonald
  Capt Kinchen's District   James Orrick

Ordered, That in all other Districts within this County, the Constables now acting continue in Office for the present year.

Ordered, That the sum of fifty four dollars be appropriated and paid to Joab Durham, for the maintenance of William Clarke, and infirm parishioner, for the year 1803. Paid.

                              Wm Rabun
                              Brice Gaither
                              Jno Wm Devereux
                              Stephen Evans
                              Thos Cooper

Court adjourned until the last Friday in this month.

Attest. Mar Martin, Clk

Friday the 27th January 1804 [95]

Court met pursuant to adjournment.

Present, their Honors   Stephen Evans }
                                     William Rabun } Esquires
                                     Thomas Cooper }

Charles Huckaby having made satisfactory proof to the Court that a Hog tolled by Isaac Hill and sold by Barnaby Shivers, Esquire was at the time of sale his right & property.

Ordered, That the sum of [blank] be paid by the Clerk to said Charles Huckaby, being the nett proceeds of Sale, after deducting legal fees.

Ordered, That Hugh Horton, Samuel Hawkins, & William Horton be and they are hereby appointed Commissioners to lay out a road the nearest and best way from Hardy Cain's landing on the Oconee river to the road leading from Sparta to the Cedar Shoals.

Iss^d H. Cain.

Friday the 27th January 1804 [96]

Ordered, That Benjamin Simmons have liberty to turn the road leading from Sparta to John Lamar's, so as to run on the South side of his Plantation, agreeably to the report of Tully Choice, John Rivers, and Arthur Fails, Commissioners appointed by order of John Coulter, Esqr to review the same.

Iss^d & given to B. Simmons' Son.

Ordered, That Randolph Rutland, Esqr be and he is hereby appointed Overseer of the road leading from Mrs Reddin's to Joseph Cooper's, ~~as far as~~ to where it intersects the road leading from Powelton to Martin Gilbert's, and that the following hands work thereon, viz.

John Butler, John Michael, John Rudisell, John Henderson, Richard Gunn, John Champion, William Lancaster, Nancy Reddin, & John Jones.

Iss^d & given to Th^o Cooper, Esqr.

Ordered, That Hardy Jernigan be and he

Friday the 27th January 1804 [97]

is hereby appointed Overseer of that part of the road leading from Mrs Reddin's to Joseph Cooper's, ~~which commences at~~ from where it intersects the road leading from Powelton to Martin Gilbert's, to the road leading from Sparta to Powelton at Joseph Cooper's Plantation, and that the following hands work thereon, viz.

Joseph Cooper, William Mathers, John Henry, Henry Graybill, James Harvey, Thomas Cooper, Frederick Tucker, James Jernigan, & Jesse Connell.

Iss^d & given Th^o Cooper, Esqr.

Ordered, That Temple Lea be and he is hereby appointed Overseer of the road from Fulsom's Creek to Stith's Mill, and that the following hands work thereon, viz.

Levi Horn, Nathan Morris, Chas Taylor, John Huckaby, Moses Brown, Greene Lea, John J. Davidson, John Smith, Ezekiel Smith, Senr, William Barfield, Greene Andrews, Gray Andrews, Drury Jackson, Andrew Stewart, John Armstrong, James Armstrong, & Reuben Jones.

Iss^d given Wm Rabun, Esqr.

Friday the 27th January 1804 [98]

Ordered, That Martin Gilbert be and he is hereby appointed Overseer of the road leading from the County line, by said Gilbert's, to the Beaverdam field, and that the following hands work thereon, viz.

Littleton Mapp, Henry Miller, Reuben Slaughter, Mrs Slaughter, John Hill, Taylor Nelson, Abner Barksdale, Joseph Barksdale, & Collier Barksdale.

Issued & given to Th^o Cooper, Esqr.

Ordered, that James Lucas be and he is hereby appointed Overseer of the road from the Beaverdam field to James Halliday's, and that the following hands do work thereon, viz.

John Harvey, Davis McGehee, Danl Connell, Henry Lucas, James Askey, Jacob Dennis, Wm Dent, Risdon Moore, Samuel Caldwell, Henry Colquit, & John Lloyd.

Iss^d gave Th^o Cooper, Esqr.

Ordered, That James Halliday be and he is

Friday the 27th January 1804 [99]

is hereby appointed Overseer of the road leading from his plantation to the Piney woods house, as far as the Powelton road, and that the following hands work thereon, viz.

John Manley, Moses Powell, Jesse Ellis, Levi Ellis, Isaac Newsom, Micajah Middlebrooks, Isaac Ellis, Salathiel Culver, Daniel Lowe, Belitha Broughton, George Culver, Thomas Worsham, & Joshua Broughton.

Iss^d gave Th^o Cooper, Esqr.

Ordered, That Wimburn Dickinson be and he is hereby appointed Overseer of the road leading from Martin Gilbert's to Powelton, as far as John Randall's plantation, and the following hands to work thereon, viz.

John Johnson, John Mason, Joseph Mason, Robert Ransom, Benjamin Rasbury, Nathan Smith, William Davenport, William Skelly, Richard Fletcher, Jonathan Moore, John Campbell, Richard Runnels, Thomas Cummins, James Cummins, Henry Long, & David Ship.

Iss^d gave Th^o Cooper, Esqr.

Friday the 27th January 1804 [100]

Ordered, That Robert Simms, Esquire be and he is hereby appointed Overseer of the road from John Randall's to the road leading from Powelton to James Harvey's, and that the following hands work thereon, viz.

John Randall, Mrs Randall, Mrs Johnson, Mrs Butler, Mrs Garrett, James Byrom, Henry Byrom, William Garrett, John Butler, Henry Butler, Randolph Rutland, Frederick Tucker, & Edmund Garrett.

Iss^d gave Th^o Cooper, Esqr.

Ordered, That the District of which Edmund Corley is Overseer be extended to the forks of the road leading to James Harvey's and John Randall's, & that the hands of John Michael, Henry Graybill, & Mrs Thompson work thereon.

Iss^d gave Th^o Cooper, Esqr.

Ordered, that Elisha Brown be and he is hereby appointed Overseer of the road from

Friday the 27th January 1804 [101]

from Town Creek to Dr Kennedy's plantation, and that the following hands work thereon, viz.

William Veals, Aaron Parker, Robert Chambers, David Chambers, Isaac Youngblood, Nathan Youngblood, Arthur Youngblood, William Youngblood, John Isle, Hardy Harrington, Ephraim Calhoun, William Pardue, John Brown, Lewis Page, [blank] Johnson, Allen Bass, & [blank] Moon.

Iss^d, Given Overseer.

Ordered, That John Graves be and he is hereby appointed Overseer of the road leading from Barksdale's Bridge on Little Ogechee to the Shoals of Ogechee, and the following hands to work thereon, viz.

Richard Morgan, Ben^j Jenkins, Robt Tate, Elisha Brothers, William Horn, Willie Jenkins, Thomas Boatwright, Daniel Wadsworth, Mark Holliman, Tisey Thomas, Lewis Graves, Jacob Duckworth, Robt Dickson, James Wadsworth, jun^r, William Wadsworth, Samuel Graves, Joel Patterson, William Cureton, Bolling Cureton, Rezin Cureton, John Cureton, John Wisener, James Wilson, Harmon Holliman, William Holliman, William Chapman, John Pullin, Henry Pullin, Saml Pullin, Thos Caswell, Richd T. Caswell, Ja^s Eppridge, Saml Thomas, John Galtney, & Thomas Miller.

iss^d, gave Tisey Thomas, Esqr.

Friday the 27th January 1804 [102]

Ordered, That Thomas Vickers be and he is hereby appointed Overseer of the road from Doctor Kennedy's to James Musselwhite's plantation, in the place of John Middlebrooks, resigned.

iss^d given said Middlebrooks.

Ordered, That Lindsay Thornton be and he is hereby appointed Overseer of the road from John Ragan's to Nathaniel Waller's plantation, in place of Hardy Smith, removed.

Iss^d [faint] Clk.

Ordered, That Bird Braswell be and he is hereby appointed Overseer of the road from George Taylor's to John Graves's, and the following hands to work thereon, viz.

Thomas Hawkins, William Newsom, John Newsom, Elijah Miller, Israel Johnson, George Taylor, Job Taylor, John Hall, David Pound, Isaac Blount, & Littleton Long.

iss^d given ~~Tisey Thomas, Esqr~~ Jeffery Barksdale.

Ordered, That that the District of road of

Friday the 27th January 1804 [103]

of which Allen Pope is Overseer be extended to Henry Moffet's old plantation, and the following hands to work thereon, viz.

Lewis Moss, Jane Bishop, Jervis Langford, & William Biggins.

Iss^d gave Wm Rabun, Esqr.

Ordered, that that the sum of thirty Dollars be appropriated and paid to Thomas Smith, a parishioner, in full for his maintenance for the year 1803.

Paid.

Ordered, that that the sum of thirty Dollars be appropriated and paid to Edward Miller, a parishioner, in full for his maintenance for the year 1804.

Paid.

Ordered, that that the sum of thirty Dollars be appropriated and paid to Drury Perkinson, an indigent person, in full for his maintenance for the year 1804.

Paid.

Ordered, that Peter Flournoy, Esqr be and he

Friday the 27th Jany 1804 [104]

he is hereby appointed a Justice of the peace in and for Capt Kinchen's District, in place of Matthew Kinchen, esquire, resigned.

Forwarded.

Ordered, that one Copy of the Report of the Commissioners of the United States on the subject of the Yazoo Sale be apportioned to each Captain's District, to each member of the Inferior Court, and to the Clerk. Those for the Districts to be delivered to one of the Justices for such District.

Ordered, That license be granted to John Stanton, to keep a house of entertainment at his residence in this County. p^d $8.00.

Ordered, That Mark Gonder have liberty to turn the road leading from Fulsom's Creek to Sparta, so as to run by his Store door.

Iss^d gave Gonder.

Friday the 27th January 1804   [105]

Ordered, that Gerard Burch, jun^r be and he is hereby appointed to take the Census in Major Horton's Battalion, agreeably to an Act of the last General Assembly.

iss^d & al C[faint]

That Willie Abercrombie be and he is hereby appointed to take the Census in Major Sanders's Battalion.

That Lazarus Battle be and he is hereby appointed to take the Census in Major Lewis Battalion, and

That Hamlin Lewis be and he is hereby appointed to take the Census in Major Davis's Battalion.

Wm Rabun
Thos Cooper
Stephen Evans

Court adjourned until the second Friday in May next.

Attest. Mar Martin, Clk

plff

Friday the 11th May 1804 [106]

Court met pursuant to adjournment.

Present, their Honors   Stephen Evans }
                               William Rabun } Esquires
                               Thomas Cooper }

Ordered, that Andrew Baxter, Walter Hamilton, Robert Clark, William Clark, & Daniel Wagnon be and they are hereby appointed Commissioners to view & lay out a road the nearest and best way from Baxter's mill on Shoulderbone to the Oconee river, near Jeremiah Thrower's plantation. Issued.

Ordered, That Moses Wiley, Esqr, Asa Alexander, and Irby Hudson be and they are hereby appointed Commissioners to view and lay out a road the nearest and best way from Capt Bixby's fence by the old Academy on Shoulderbone to Asa Alexander's plantation. Issued.

Friday the 11th May 1804 [107]

Ordered, that the road ~~leading~~ contemplated to lead from Miles's Store to Thaddeus Holt's mill on Town Creek, agreeably to an order of Court of the 6th June 1803, be and the same is hereby discontinued.

Solomon Ellis }
      vs   }
Joseph B. Jones }

On the Petition of defendant, stating that he is confined in the common Jail of this County at the Suits of Solomon Ellis, & praying the benefit of the Acts for the relief of insolvent debtors, it is

Ordered, that the third Saturday in July next be assigned for said Jones to be brought into Court to enquire into his insolvency, and that a Copy of this rule be served on the plaintiff, or his Attorney, and published in the Savannah or Augusta Gazette at least two months previous to the said third Saturday in July next, of which all the Creditors of said Joseph B. Jones will take notice.

It appearing to the Court that the plff in

Friday the 11th May 1804 [108]

in this case failed or neglected to give bond & Sec^y for the weekly payment of the Jail fees &c, on ~~Motion of Defendant's counsel~~ application of the Jailor, it is

Ordered, that the said Joseph B. Jones be discharged from his confinement.

Malachi Jones }
    vs }
Joseph B. Jones }

It appearing to the Court that the defendant is confined in the common Jail of this County, and that the plaintiff had failed to give bond & Sec^y for the weekly payment of the Jail fees &c, on application, it is

Ordered, that the Defendant be discharged from his confinement.

Ordered, That the sum of thirty three dollars be & the same is hereby appropriated & paid to Saml Hall, Coroner, in full for holding an Inquest on the bodies of Absalom Saunders, George Chetam, & an Inquest & funeral expenses for a child supposed to be Judy Higginbotham's.

Friday the 11th May 1804 [109]

Ordered, That John Latimore be & he is hereby appointed Overseer of the road leading from Stith's road to Fulsom's ford on Ogechee, through Humphries's lane, between Mark Gonder's (late Ben^j Cook's) & Saml Barron's plantation, in place of James Miller, resigned, and that the following hands work thereon, viz.

George Latimore, James Tilman, William Willis, Thomas Willis, Robert Latimore, Maston Pruit, Jesse Izzel, David Clark, Samuel Howell, Meshach Howell, Matthew Humphries, William Humphries, Nathan Simpson, & Robt Hicks. Issued.

Ordered, That Zephaniah Harvey & William Saunders be and they are hereby appointed Commissioners to lett to the lowest bidder the building of a bridge across Buffalo creek, at the Widow Hunter's plantation, & the same to kept in repair five years. Issued.

Ordered, That John Lucas be and he is hereby appointed Overseer of the road from Sparta to

Friday the 11th May 1804 [110]

to George Cowin's plantation, in place of John Freeman, resigned. Issued.

Ordered, That Jeremiah Walker be and he is hereby appointed Overseer of the road from Montpellier Warehouse to Derry's creek, in place of David Hubert, resigned. Issued.

Ordered, That William Saunders be and he is hereby appointed Overseer of the road leading from Mrs Hunter's plantation to Eiland's Mill on Buffalo, and that the following hands do work thereon, viz.

James Cain, Job Jackson, John Norsworthy, John Moy, Mr Stephens, William Saunders, Barnaby Pope, William McDowell, John Cain, John Donnaghey, John L. Jones, Nehemiah Harvey, Zephaniah Harvey, Wm Brodnax, Edwd B. Brodnax, Ben^j Temple, Drury Musselwhite, Robt Stell, Wm Harvey, Saml Lancaster, Eph^m Whittington, Wm Carter, James Carter, Jesse Carter, Wm Pate, Williamson Johnson, Saml Johnson, Gab^l Moffet, John Moffet, Chas Johnson, Jacob Earnest, & Isaac Wilson.

Friday the 11th May 1804 [111]

Ordered, That Hartwell Garey be and he is hereby appointed Overseer of the road from Sparta to the Widow Hunter's plantation, in place of James Pinkston, removed. Issued.

Ordered, That Thomas Mathews, Allen Bass, & Arthur Youngblood be & they are hereby appointed Commissioners to view & lay out a road the nearest and best way from Lindsay Roberts's, by Jacob Dennis's Mill, so as to join the road from Sparta to Mitchell's old Store, near said Store. Issued.

Ordered, That James Simmons be and he is hereby appointed Overseer of the road from Joseph Cooper's Mill on Logdam to Parham's Mill on Fort creek, and that the following hands do work thereon, viz.

Thomas C. Butts, Fred^k Butts, John Weeks, Thomas Lancaster, Joseph Cooper, Thos Clark,

Friday the 11th May 1804 [112]

James Rae, Quinney Powell, Jethro Jackson, Thomas Henson, Thomas Johnson, Jacob Lockett, Alex^r Bass, Senr, Jesse Warren, John Sturdivant, Myles Greene, Ge^o Smith, Daniel Melson, Allen Hudson, Wm Sharpe, Lewis Saunders, Fra^s Moreland, Robt Moreland, Jesse McKinney Pope, Th^o Simmons, George Simmons, Robt Parham, William Love, Andrew Love, Robert Simmons, & James Childs. Issued.

Ordered, That Wyatt Collier be & he is hereby appointed Overseer of the road from Parham's Mill to the Sparta road, in place of Lewis Barnes, deceased. Issued.

Ordered, That Philip Turner be & he is hereby appointed Overseer of the

Friday the 11th May 1804 [113]

the road from the Stony ridge to the old County line, in place of James Hall, resigned.

Wm Rabun
Thos Cooper
Stephen Evans

Court adjourned until Court in Course.

Mar Martin, Clk

Monday the 4th June 1804 [114]

Court met pursuant to adjournment.

Present, their Honors   William Rabun   }
                        Stephen Evans & } Esquires
                        Thomas Cooper   }

Ordered, That Tavern license be granted to George Gray, to keep a house of entertainment at his residence in this County. rec^d $9.56¼.

Ordered, That John Miles be and he is hereby appointed first Inspector, Tilman Buckner Second, & Alexander Greene third Inspector of Tobacco at Montpellier Warehouse.

Ordered, That the sum of thirty one dollars eighty Seven & an half Cents be appropriated and paid to John Freeman, in full for the Jail fees of William Wells. Issued.

Monday the 4th June 1804 [115]

Ordered, That license be granted to Vines Harwell, William Hudson, & Samuel Beall, to keep houses of entertainment at their respective residences in this County.

rec^d $28.56. rec^d $28.68¾ for all.

Ordered, That a tax equal to one fifth part of the General Tax be levied for County purposes.

Ordered, That Uriah Thweatt, Esquire do shew cause, if any he hath to shew, why an attachment should not issue against him for the Jail fees and costs of suit in the Case of Solomon Ellis vs Joseph B. Jones, and that he a Copy of this order be served on him before the third Friday in next month, at which time he is to answer to this order.

Jno Wm Devereux
Stephen Evans
Wm Rabun
Thos Cooper

Friday the 7th September 1804 [116]

Court met pursuant to Adjournment.

Present, their Honors   Jno Wm Devereux }
                        Wm Rabun &   } Esquires
                        Richard A. Blount }

Ordered, That William H. Matthers have liberty to alter the road leading from Powelton to Sparta, agreeably to Report of Henry Graybill, Joseph Henry, & William Lee, Esquires.

Ordered, That Andrew Stewart have liberty to turn the publick Road leading from Sparta to Stith's Mill, Agreeable to the report of Ezekiel Smith, Richard Shipp, and Drury Jackson, commissioners appointed to review Said road.

Ordered, That the following persons be subject to work on the road leading from the old County line to Little Ogeechee Bridge, to wit.

Martin Armstrong, Benjamin Thompson, Overoff

Friday 7th September 1804 [117]

Jordan, Isham Huckaby, James Wilkerson, James Majers, James Walker, Reuben Walker, Thomas Lovett, Phillip Bailey, Samuel Walding, Giles Kelley, Peter Boyle, Joab Durham, James Casstleburry, Richard A. Blount, James Wood, Edmond Beard, Solomon Phillips, James Shye, Alexander Herring, John Patterson, Jesse Page, Samuel John, Daniel Grantham, Starling Ammons, John Turner, David Thomas, & Francis Lewis, James Page, Overseer. iss^d.

Ordered, that Joseph Porter be & he is hereby appointed Overseer of that part of the road leading from Fort Wilkerson to Holt's Mills, where the Washington County line crosses the same. issued.

Ordered, that John Montgomery be & he is hereby appointed Overseer of the road leading from Sparta to Montpellier, for that part between Bivins's and Montpellier, in the room of Samuel Parker. iss^d.

Ordered, that Allen Green be & he is hereby appointed Overseer of the road leading from

Friday 7th September 1804 [118]

Montpellier to Borland's Mill, that David Hubert was formerly Overseer. And that the Same hands be Subject to work thereon. iss^d.

Ordered, that Tavern license be granted to William Beavin, Edmond Beard, & Richard H. Carew, to keep houses of entertainment at their respective places of residence.

E. Beard p^d $9.56¼.

Ordered, that Randolph Rutland be and he is hereby appointed a Justice of the Peace in Capt Connill's Dis^t, in place of William Dent, Senr, Esquire, resigned.

Ordered, that Allen Bass be & he is hereby appointed a Justice of the Peace in Capt Minor's District, in place of Seth Kennedy, removed.

Wm Rabun
Jno Wm Devereux
Richard A. Blount

Court Adjourned until the Second friday in November next.

Ja^s Lewis, Clk

Saturday the 8th September 1804   [119]

Ordered, that Tavern license be granted to William Sanford & John Pearson, to keep houses of entertainment at their respective places of residence.

p^d $9.56¼ p^d $9.56¼

Wm Rabun
Jno Wm Devereux
Richard A. Blount

Ordered, that Wm Biggins & Jonathan Davis be appointed Coms^{rs}, to join those of Warren County, to let to the lowest bidder the building and keeping in repair the bridge across Ogechee at Stith's Mill for five years.

Friday November 9th 1804

The Honorable Richard A. Blount and Thomas Cooper met agreeable to Adjournment, but not forming a quorum, they could not proceed to business, therefore adjourned until friday the 14th December next.

James Lewis, Clk

Friday December 14th 1804 [120]

Court met pursuant to adjournment.

Present, their Honors   Stephen Evans }
                             Jnº Wm Devereux } Esquires
                             Wm Rabun }

Ordered, that the sum of fifty eight dollars be appropriated & paid to Benjamin J. Borden, for building a Bridge across Buffalo at the Widow Hunter's.

Pd 2nd March 1805.

Ordered, that the following hands be subject to work on the road leading from Baxter's Mills on Shoulderbone to the Oconee river at Jeremiah Thrower's, Viz.

Edward Clanton, John Bishop, Joseph Chappel, James Farley, Elizabeth Sledge, Chappel Sledge, John Sledge, Phillimon Foster, James Singleton, Phillip Barnhart, John Foster's sons, Benjamin Anderson, Thomas Clower, John Lowe, Wm Clower, John Taylor, Lewis Smith, John Low, junr, David Adams, Daniel Lowe, Colston Heath, Chappel Heath, Stephen Evans, Jere Thrower, Noah Dodrige,

Friday December 14th 1804 [121]

and Henry Clark.

And it is further Ordered, that Daniel Wagnon be and he is hereby appointed Overseer of the Same.

Ordered, that the following hands be subject to work on the road leading from Sparta to the Widow Hunter's plantation, Viz.

Robert Raines, John Turner, Smith Cotton, Jas Baker, Jesse Baker, Senr, Wm Stembridge, Hubbard Bonner, Jas Bonner, Thos M. Bonner, Richard Bonner, David Pinkerton, Benjn J. J. Birdon, Richard Sasnett, John Wilkerson, John Pinkston, Greenberry Pinkston. And that Hartwell Garey be Overseer.

Ordered, that Benjamin Parker be & he is hereby appointed Overseer of that part of the road leading from Buffaloe bridge to Booth's Mount, & from Mitchel's

Store to Moore's Shop (white plains) and that the same hands be subject to work on said road that were pointed out to work with the former Overseer. issued.

Ordered, that the following work on the road from Bivins' to Montpellier, Viz.

Jonathan Colbert, Arch Terrell, Mrs Cathell, Ann Miles, John Conner, Dempsey Justice, James Miles, George Simpson, James Montgomery, David Montgomery,

Friday December 14th 1804   [122]

Michael Rogers, Alex^r Greene, Robert Hill, Saml Kirkpatrick, Ransom Lea, Samuel Parker, Levin Cathell, Wm Montgomery, Thomas Talbert, Silas Talbert, Jacob Buckholts, William Buckholts, Samuel Slaughter, Daniel Slaughter, Jeremiah Miles, Isaiah Chapman, Benj^a Buchannan, Widow Miles, Phillip Levare, William Justice, Isaiah Chapman, Marlow Prior, Thomas Taylor, Lewis May, & John Prior.

Ordered, that the following hands be Subject to work on the road leading from Asa Alexander's down to Capt Bishop's, Viz.

Asa Alexander, Thos Hill, Green Cato, John Wilkerson, Ja^s Wilkerson, Aron Yarnell, Danl Yarnel, Daniel Orear, John Orear, Senr, Wm Orear, Richd Moon, Wood Moreland, Saml Mattox, James Moon, James Barnes, Demsey Wright, Peter Dent, & Levi Daniel, Overseer.

Ordered, That the following hands be subject to work on the road leading from the old ridge road to Hudson's Mill, Viz.

Irby Hudson, William Hudson, Benjamin Cornelius, Robt Kelly,

Friday December 14th 1804   [123]

Jeremiah Nelson, George Nelson, John Luckey, Jacob Goore, Marium Orear, Joseph Loyd, Sterling Lewis, Archibald Lewis, John Dudley, Jacob Moman, Robert Gilbert, Seth Tatum, Nathl Barksdale, John Kelly, Benj^a Woodruff, Thos Scott, Woodlief Scott, Robert Holt, Nicholas Robbins, Robert Mitchell, Nicholas Dickson, Robert Harrison, ~~& Nathan Daniel, Overseer,~~ & Thomas Little, Overseer of the same.

Ordered, that the following hands be Subject to work on the road leading from ~~Hudson's~~ the creek below Hudson's Mill, to the road that leads from Obadiah Richardson's to Sparta, at the corner of Capt Bishop's plantation, Viz.

Amos Daniel, James Barnes, Joseph Barnes, Absalom Barnes, Nathan Barnes, Jesse Barnes, Abel Barnes, Green Wynne, Thos Wynne, Lemon Barnes, Thos Cates, Ge^o Parker, Wm Tyus, John Dickerson, Jesse Mattox, Alexander Mattox, Wm Giles,

Friday December 14th 1804   [124]

Samuel Kindrick, Hezekiah Kindrick, Richard Joels, Simon Holt, Senr, Edward Brodnax, & Nathan Daniel, Overseer of the Same.

Ordered, that Jeffrey Edwards, James Edwards, Richard Edwards, Loraney Edwards, William Edwards, & Sally Edwards, children of a certain Woman of colour called free Cate, be bound to Joseph Turner, jun^r, until they arive to lawful age.

Ordered, that the Sum of ten Dollars be appropriated & paid to Samuel Hall, for holding an inquest over the body of Ward Daniell. Paid 3rd Ap^l 1805.

Ordered, that the following hands be subject to work on the road leading from Eilands' Mill to Mitchell's Store at the levels, Viz.

Absalom Eilands, Asa Eilands, Enoch Eilands, Benjamin Morris, John Lowe, Thomas Jones, Thomas Matthews, Allen Bass, William Foreson, Meshack Hitchcock, Jonathan Youngblood, & Arthur Youngblood, Overseer.

Friday December 14th 1804   [125]

Ordered, that Tavern license be granted Jared Birch, J^r & Dennis Doyle, to keep houses of entertainment at their respective places of residence in this County.

Ordered, that the Sum of thirty Six dollars be appropriated & paid to Mrs Henriken. in full for the maintenance of Thomas McFarling, an Orphan Child, commencing the 27th January last.

Ordered, that John Lattimer be & he is hereby appointed a Justice of the Peace in Capt Lattimer's District, in place of John Andrews, resigned.

Ordered, that Henry Dixon be & he is hereby appointed a Justice of the Peace in Capt Holt's District, in place of Singleton Holt, resigned.

That Risdon Moore, Senr be & he is hereby appointed a Justice of the Peace in Capt Connill's Dis^t, in place of Randolph Rutland, who refuses to qualify.

Friday December 14th 1804   [126]

Ordered, that John Matthews be & he is hereby appointed a Justice of the Peace in Capt Graybill's Dis^t, in place of Robert Rivers, resigned.

Ordered, that the following hands be subject to work on the road leading from George Cowen's to Obadiah Richardson's, viz.

James Bishop, Joseph Bryan, Dixon Hall, Senr, Hugh Hall, Peterson Thweatt, John Manley, Wm Willey, ~~Littleton~~ & Francis Daney, & Littleton Reese, Overseer.

Jno W. Devereux
Wm Rabun
Stephen Evans

Court adjourned until Court in course.

James Lewis, Clk

Monday the 7th January 1805   [127]

Court met Pursuant to adjournment.

Present, their Honors   Stephen Evans }
                                      William Rabun } Esq^{rs}
                                      Jno Wm Devereux }

John Crowder, Esquire produced his Commission and took the oath proscribed by the Constitution & took his seat accordingly.

The Court and Justices of the Peace attended, proceeded to the election of a receiver of Tax returns & Collector of Taxes for the present year, & on closing the polls, it appeared that John Comer, Esquire was duly elected receiver of Tax returns & Leonard Abercrombie, Esquire Collector of Taxes.

Ordered, that Tavern License be granted to Thomas Crowder & C° & Sampson Duggar, to keep houses of entertainment at their respective places of residence. Paid $19.12½.

Monday the 7th January 1805 [128]

Ordered, that the following Constables be & they are hereby appointed for the respective Districts following, Viz.

 For Capt Simmon's District, John Wilson
 For Capt Brown's D° Nathaniel Waller, jun^r
 " Capt Lewis's District, John Rivers
 " Capt Barksdale's District, John Brown
 " Capt Slocum's District, William Harvy & Curtis Hay
 " Capt Bass's, James Orrick
 " Capt Simmons' Powelton, John Colbert & Wm Lord
 " Capt Graybill's District, Christian Patrick
 " Capt Huff's District, Nicholas Dixon & William Mills

And that all other appointments of Constables in other Districts in this County, who are now acting, be & they are hereby continued.

Monday the 7th January 1805 [129]

Ordered, that the following Tavern rates be taken this year, and no more, Viz.

Jamaica Rum, Holland Gin, Cognac, brandy, 4th proof by the half pint	$0.25
West India Rum, North^d Gin, 3rd proof, Claret, port, or Sherry Wine by the half pint	$0.18¾
Northard Rum, Peach or apple Brandy, or whisky first proof Malaga Teneriff & C° Wine, the ½ pint	0.12½
Cyder or Malt Beer by the quart	0.12½
Diet for breakfast or Supper	0.25
Dinner	0.25

Lodging	0.06¼
Forrage by the feed, 3 qts corn or clean Oats & fodder	0.12½
Stabling & feed night & morning in proportion	0.37½

Monday the 7th January 1805 [130]

Ordered, that the poll Tax of Charles Huckaby, Senr be & the same is hereby remitted.

Ordered, that the Sum of thirty two dollars Sixty five & one quarter cents be appropriated & paid to Hugh Taylor, in full for the proportion of Hancock County for repairing the bridge at George Town, agreeable to the following Statement, Viz. the general Tax for Hancock is three thousand & twenty Six dollars fourteen & half cents, for Warren County one thousand five hundred twenty three dollars & fifty four cents, & the County of Washington fourteen hundred & Seventy four dollars thirty five & half Cents

Monday the 7th January 1805 [131]

Ordered, that Uriah Askey be Overseer of the road from William H. Matthers's to the road leading from James Halliday's to the piney woods house, and that Wm Alford, Senr, Wm Alford, Junr, Benjamin Leonard, Owen Alford, Joseph Cooper, Senr, & Charles Sturdivant do work on the same.

Ordered, that Tavern License be granted to John Freeman, to keep a house of entertainment at his place of residence in Sparta.

Ordered, that Hugh M. Comer be and he is hereby appointed a Justice of the Peace in Capt Graybill's District, in the place of Jno Cook, Esqr, resigned.

Ordered, that John Turner be and he is hereby appointed a Justice of the Peace for Capt Barksdale's district, in place of Barnaby Shivers, ~~resigned~~ removed.

Monday the 7th January 1805 [132]

Ordered, that Thos Scott be and he is hereby appointed a Justice of the Peace for Capt Hudson's District, in place of Saml Dent, removed.

Ordered, that John Freeman & Duke Hamilton be and they are hereby Appointed Justices of the Peace in Capt Barnes' District, in place of Arch^d M. Devereux & Jno Crowder, Esqr, resigned.

Jno Crowder
Stephen Evans
Wm Rabun

Court adjourned until the third friday in this month.

Ja^s Lewis, Clk

Friday 8th February 1805 [133]

Court met pursuant to ajournment.

Present, their Honors   Stephen Evans }
                         William Rabun } Esquires
                         John Crowder }

Ordered, that Samuel Shi be and he is hereby appointed Overseer of the road leading from Edmund Beard's to Benjamin Averett's, and that the following hands work thereon, viz.

William John, Robert Montgomery, William Grantham, Richard Perkins, Uriah Perkins, James Logue, Richard Jarnett, John Dunn, Isaac Dennis, jun^r, John McKay, Benjamin Chapman, Ezekiel Boman, William Gilliland, Moses Boman, William Williams, John Brown, Major Peace, David Huckaby, Richd Huckaby, Alexander McCook, & Robert McCook.

Ordered, that Tavern license be granted to Captain Samuel Hall of Sparta, to keep a house of entertainment.

Friday 8th February 1805 [134]

Ordered, that Tavern license be granted to Captain John Burch of Powelton, to keep a house of entertainment. [faint]

Ordered, that the sum of ten Dollars be appropriated and paid to Captain Samuel Hall, for holding an inquest of the body of Thomas Dollard, late of this County, deceased. Paid.

Ordered, that Wright Hill be and he is hereby appointed Overseer of that part of the road, Viz. from the cross roads at William Gay's to Job Taylor's, and that the following hands work thereon, Viz.

Amos Brantley, William Williams, Micajah Pickard, Charles Stewart, William Seales, George Allen, John Miller (B. Smith), William Murphey, Job Taylor, George Taylor, Isaac Morgan, and John Murphey.

Ordered, that Tavern license be granted to Allen and James Greene, to keep a house of entertainment at Montpellier (Miles Greene, Esqr, Security for the condemnation money). $9.56¼

Friday 8th February 1805 [135]

Ordered, that the following persons be subject to work on the road leading from the mouth of Mrs Tison's lane to ~~Chambers's~~ Baxter's mill road, leading from Sparta, (Viz.)

John Peterson, Duke Hamilton, John Crowder, Epps Brown, John C. Peak, Henry Mitchell, Frederick Echols, & John McLemore, & John Peak, jun^r, Overseer of the Same. issued.

Ordered, that Jesse Foreman, an Orphan Child, be bound to John Bishop until he becomes of Lawful age.

Ordered, that the following hands work on the road leading from Shoulderbone Bridge Baxter's Mill to Greene County line, Viz.

William Mills, James Huff, Robt Adams, Robert Middlebrooks, Mark Moon, Stith Evans, David Evans, Abner Evans, Henry Furguson, James Wooton, Thomas Walker, David Walker, William Walker, Greene Cato, John Hern, Chappell Heath, Walter Hamilton, James Lyon, David Adams, Peyton Sledge, Green Wood, Wm Adams, [blank] Gary, Benjamin Parrott, John Thomas,

Friday 8th February 1805 [136]

Isaac Motley, & Thomas Middlebrooks, and that Isaac Motley be Overseer of the Same.

Ordered, that Tavern license be granted to Jeremiah Thrower, to Keep a House of entertainment at his place of residence in this County. p^d $9.56¼.

Ordered, that Samuel White be & he is hereby appointed overseer of the road leading from Shadrack Roe's to North Fort Creek. issued.

Ordered, that Walter Hamilton, Robert Clark, & John Bishop be & they are hereby appointed Commissioners to let to the lowest bidder the building of a bridge a cross Shoulderbone at Baxter's Mill. iss^d.

> Wm Rabun
> Jno Crowder
> Stephen Evans

Court Adjourned until the third friday in March next.

Attest. Ja^s Lewis, Clk

Friday March the 15th 1805 [137]

Court met pursuant to Adjournment.

Present, their Honors   William Rabun   }
                               Richard A. Blount } Esq^{rs}
                               John Crowder &   }
                               Stephen Evans   }

Thomas & Wm Smith }
& D. Anderson   }
      vs   } Cas Sa
John Wilson   }

Ordered, that the defendant be brought up instanter to hear what the Court may determine in his favor.

Ordered, that Joel Newsom be bound to Isaac Newsom [blot] until he becomes of lawful Age.

Rule Nisi

On the Petition of William Low, Stating that he was possessed of two several Notes of hand, they both bearing date the Eighth of September in the year Seventeen Hundred and ninety Six, which said Notes were made payable on the twenty fifth day of December in the year Seventeen hundred and ninety Seven, by

Joseph Smith to William Ingram, the one of said Notes for one hundred dollars, the other for three hundred dollars

Friday the 15th of March 1805 [138]

dollars, which said Notes of hand were endorsed to your Petitioner by the said William Ingram, Copies of which said Notes are filed with the Vouchers required by Law (with an affidavit that the said Notes were lost) agreeable to an Act of Assembly in such Cases made & provided. It is ordered, that the said Notes be established as directed by the said Act. And the said William Low's publishing, as therein required, for the space of Six months in one of the public Gazettes of this State, unless cause be shewn to the contrary within the said Months, other Matters shall appear to the Court against the same.

Thomas & Wm Smith }
& D. Anderson }
    vs   } Ca Sa
John Wilson }

On the Petition of John Wilson, praying to be discharged as an insolvent Debtor.

Ordered, that the thirtieth day of March be the day on which the said John Wilson will be brought into Court to enquire into his Insolvency, of which all his Creditors will take Notice.

Friday the 15th of March 1805 [139]

Ordered, that Tavern License be granted to Isaac Hill, Senr & Mark Gonder, to Keep houses of entertainment at their respective places of residence in this County. paid.

Ordered, that Tavern License be granted to John J. Davidson, to Keep a house of entertainment at his place of residence in this County. paid.

On the Petition of Sundry inhabitants of this County.

Ordered, that a former Order of this Court for the opening of a road from Montpellier to the mouth of Shoulderbone be revoked, it appearing to the Court that said road will not be of public Utility. iss^d.

Ordered, that Samuel Dent have liberty to turn the public road leading from Baxter's Mills to Thrower's ferry on the Oconee River (Viz.) leaving the present road at Winslet's fork of Shoulderbone, from thence up s^d Creek, Keeping the best ground to the lane between said Dent & J. Bishop, thence along Dent's line to a branch near Joseph Chappell's, from thence a direct course into the present road where s^d Chappell's line crosses the same, agreeable to the Report of the Commissioners.

Friday March the 15th 1805 [140]

Ordered, that Lester Buckner, an orphan child, be bound to John Buckner, until he becomes of lawful Age.

Ordered, that Morris & Richmond Buckner, orphan children, be bound to Joel Buckner, until they become of lawful Age.

Ordered, that Samuel Pope be & he is hereby appointed overseer of the road leading from fulsom's Creek to James Evans's, in place of Mark Gonder, resigned.

Ordered, that John Smith be & he is hereby appointed overseer of the road leading from Nathaniel Waller's to Charles McDonald's, in place of Linsy Thornton, removed.

Ordered, that Tavern license be granted to Phillip Turner, to Keep a House of entertainment at his Place of residence in Sparta.

Ordered, that the following Sums be appriated & paid to the following persons (Viz.)

To   Richard Tamison ~~Eight~~ Thirty Dollars ~~& Sixty Cents~~

"   Thomas Smith ~~Eight~~ Thirty Dollars ~~& Thirty Cents~~

"   ~~Thomas~~ Edward Miller ~~Eight~~ Thirty Dollars ~~& Thirty Cents~~

"   Sarah Musselwhite ~~Eight~~ twenty dollars ~~& twenty Cents~~

"   Martha Martin One hundred dollars as indigent Persons

Paid.

Friday the 15th of March 1805 [141]

Ordered, that the Sum of fifty Dollars be appropriated and paid to John Peace, in full for the maintenance of John Mitchell the last year as an indigent Person. Paid.

Ordered, that the Sum of thirty dollars be Appropriated & paid to Mrs Herrikin for Keeping an Orphan Child to commence the 27th January last for one year. Paid $15.00.

> Wm Rabun
> Stephen Evans
> Richard Blount
> Jn° Crowder

Ordered, that Tavern License be granted to William Stanton, to Keep a House of entertainment at his place of residence in this County. paid.

> Stephen Evans
> Jn° W. Devereux
> Richard Blount
> Jn° Crowder

Saturday the 16th of March 1805 [142]

Ordered, that Betsey Worsham, an orphan Child, be bound to Collin Pope until She becomes of lawful age.

Ordered, that Anna Worsham, an orphan Child, be bound to John Trippe until she becomes of lawful age.

Ordered, that James Jewel, an orphan Child, be bound to Frederick Echols until he becomes of lawful age

Ordered, that Thomas Brantly be & he is hereby appointed Overseer of the road leading from Baxter's Mill along by John Gay's, in place of Dudly Hargrove, resigned, & the usual hands to work on the Same.

$$\begin{array}{l}\text{W}^\text{m}\text{ Rabun}\\\text{Jn}^\text{o}\text{ Crowder}\\\text{Jn}^\text{o}\text{ W. Devereux}\\\text{Stephen Evans}\\\text{Rich}^\text{d}\text{ Blount}\end{array}$$

Court Adjourned until the 30$^\text{th}$ In$^\text{t}$.

Ja$^\text{s}$ Lewis, Clk

Hancock Inferior Court 1$^\text{st}$ April 1805 [143]

Present their Honors   William Rabun   }
                         John Crowder   } Esq$^\text{rs}$
                         Richard A. Blount }

Ordered that the following sums be appropriated and paid to Jesse Grigg, esquire, for and in behalf of the following Persons, Viz.

To Henry Darnell 50 Cents	$0.50
" Joseph Biggam 50 d$^\text{o}$	0.50
" Francis Biggam	0.50
" Thomas Lancaster	0.50
" Charles Kennedy	0.50
" Frederick Truman	0.50
" Dennis L. Ryan	0.50
" Andrew Collins	1.00
" Patrick Carten	1.00
" Dennis Doyle	0.50
" Edward Welch	1.00
Carried forward	$7.00

Monday 1$^\text{st}$ April 1805 [144]

Amount brot forward	$7.00
To Solomon Rountree	0.50
" Jacob Tood	1.00

" Epps Moss	0.50
" James Moss	1.00
" Jesse Cooksey	0.50
" Stewart Anderson	0.50
" Frederick Sanford	4.50
" Philip Turner	0.50
" Wm Sandf^d & Alex Martin 50 cts each Paid A M	16.00
Amounting to seventeen dollars as compensation for their	1.00

Services in guarding the Jail during the confinement of Robert Munroe, William Cases, & Barnaby Parr. Paid.

Thomas Smith   }
William Smith &   }
Douglass Anderson }
    vs   } Ca Sa
John Wilson   }

The defendant, having given in a Schedule of all his property to this Court, it is Ordered, that the said Defendant shall deliver all and Singular the property contained in the Said Schedule into the hands

Monday 1st April 1805   [145]

hands of the Sheriff. And that he give bond and security for the delivery thereof, until delivered, and that he be from thenceforth discharged from confinement.

                                  Wm Rabun
                                  Jno Crowder
                                  Richard Blount

Court adjourned till the second Friday in May.

Attest. Alex Martin, pro Clk

Friday the 12th of April 1805   [146]

Present, their Honors   John W. Devereux }
                                          Richard A. Blount } Esq^{rs}
                                          & John Crowder }

Ordered, that Benjamin Huckaby be bound to James Page, until he becomes of lawful age.

Ordered, that Charles Huckaby be bound to James Pinkston, until he becomes of lawful Age.

Ordered, that the following hands be Subject to work on the Road leading from the old County line to Edmond Beard's (Viz.)

Martin Armstrong, Benj^a Thompson, Henry Hill, Ja^s Majors, Ja^s Walker, Reuben Walker, Joab Durham, Ja^s Wilkerson, Ja^s Shy, Ed Beard, and that Samuel Walden be Overseer of the Same.

Friday the 12th of April 1805 [147]

Ordered, that the following hands be Subject to work on the road from Edmond Beard's to little Ogeechee (Viz.)

Francis Lewis, Richard A. Blount, James Wood, Jno Patterson, Alex^r Herring, John Fagan, Jesse Page, James Page, Danl John, Danl Grantham, Stephen Fulgham, Henry Crowel, Henry Griffin, Davis Smith, Jiles Kelly, Solomon Phillips, and that Sterling Ammons be Overseer of the Same.

$\qquad\qquad\qquad\qquad$ Jno W. Devereux
$\qquad\qquad\qquad\qquad$ Richard Blount
$\qquad\qquad\qquad\qquad$ Jno Crowder

Court Adjourned until Court in Course.

Ja^s Lewis, Clk

Friday 10th May 1805 [148]

The Court met agreeable to adjournment.

Present,$\qquad\qquad\qquad\qquad$ William Rabun }
$\qquad\qquad\qquad\qquad\qquad\;\;$ Richd A. Blount } Esq^{rs}
$\qquad\qquad\qquad\qquad\qquad\;\;$ & John Crowder }

Ordered, That John Broadnax do and he is hereby authorized to receive five hundred dollars from the County funds for the building & keeping in repair a Bridge across Shoulderbone at Baxter's Mills for five years. $100 p^d.

Ordered, That Sampson Duggar and Edmond Conley be and they are hereby appointed Commissioners to let to the lowest bidder the building and keeping in repair for five years a Bridge over the Ogeechee at Lucas' Mill.

Ordered, That John Goodson be and he is hereby bound as an Apprentice to Jeremiah Averett.

Friday 10th May 1805 [149]

Upon the Petition of Ichabud Nelson, praying the benefits of the Act of Insolvency.

Ordered, That the 11th day of May be the day on which the said Ichabud Nelson will be brought into Court to enquire into his Insolvency, of which all his creditors will take notice.

Ordered, That John Freeman receive out of the County funds eight dollars and seventy five Cents, for Jail expenses.

Ordered, That the Road leading from Devereux's Mill to Doct^r Kenedy's be discontinued.

Ordered, That the Clerk of this Court be and he is hereby required to Certify the receipt of the Books of the Receiver of Tax Returns of this County for the year 1803.

Friday 10th May 1805 [150]

Ordered, That Thomas Mathews and Jacob Dennis be and they are hereby appointed overseers to the Road leading from Dennis's Mill, of the road leading from Mitchell's old Store. And that the following hands work on the Road, to wit.

John Middlebrooks	Peter Dennis
Cader Powel	Nathl Perminter
Thos Jones	William Johnson

John Low   Allen Bass
William Dennis

                            Wm Rabun
                            J^{no} Crowder
                            Richard Blount

Court adjourned until May 11th.

                Saturday 11th May 1805   [151]

Court met agreeable to adjournment.

Present,   William Rabun   }
                            Richard A. Blount } Esq^{rs}
                            & John Crowder   }

Ordered, That Isaac Battle be and he is hereby appointed overseer of the Road leading from Nancy Redding's to Powelton, and that the following hand work on the same, to wit.

        Michael Harvey, Senr   William Lord
        Pinkey Harvey   Needham Jernigan
        Nathaniel Bell   Jesse Bell
        James Jernigan   Isaac Battle
        Nancy Champion   Jesse Smith
        Solomon Jordan   John Henderson

Ordered, That Joseph Roberts be and he is hereby appointed overseer of the Road leading from Gerard Burches Mill to Powelton, and that the following persons be subject to work on the same, to wit.

Daniel D. Smith, John Ingram, Nicholas Darby, John Lee, Senr, Daniel Blankenship,

                Saturday 11th May 1805   [152]

William Northarn, Sion West, Gerard Burch, Senr, Isaac Morgan, Joseph Roberts, Samuel Mitchell, John Mitchell, Daniel Mitchell, William Pommirson, and Kinchen Hall.

Ordered, That Thomas Crowder be and he is hereby appointed a Justice of the Peace in Captain Brown's district, in place of William Lee, Esquire, resigned.

Rule Nisi

Georgia } Inferior Court
Hancock County } Chambers 11th May 1805

Upon the Petition of Abram Rowles, Stating that he was possessed of a Note of hand, given by Robert Greene and James lane Jones to him for twenty dollars & thirty seven Cents, bearing date the fifth day of February Eighteen hundred and five, copy of which said Note, with the necessary Vouchers, are filed as required by Law, together with an affidavit that the Said note was destroyed, Agreeable to an Act Assembly

Saturday 11th May 1805 [153]

such cases made and provided.

Ordered, That the said Note be established as directed by said ~~note~~ act, on the Said Abram Rawles publishing as therein required for the Space of Six Months in one of the public Gazettes of this state, unless Cause be Shewn to the Contrary within the said Six Months, or other Matters shall appear to the Court against the same.

Ordered, That Benjamin Cook receive out of the County funds two hundred and sixty six dollars & fifty Cents, as the proportionable part of Hancock County for building a Bridge over the Ogeechee at Shivers' Mill.

Wm Rabun
Richard Blount
Jno Crowder

Wednesday the 5th June 1805 [154]

Present, their Honors   William Rabun }
                             Stephen Evans & } Esq^{rs}
                             Richard A. Blount }

June Term 1805

At a former Term (To wit) at January Term 1805, the Court having heard the petition of Joseph B. Jones, praying to be discharged as an Insolvent Debtor, & the said Joseph B. Jones having taken the necessary oath & produced a Receipt from the Sheriff for the property named in his Schedule.

Ordered, that the said Joseph B. Jones be discharged in terms of the Act entitled an Act for the relief of Insolvent Debtors.

Ordered, that the Sum of ten dollars be appropriated to the use of the Widow of Thomas Smith, Dec^d. paid.

Ordered, that tavern License be granted to John Mitchell, Eli Harris & Co, & Thweatts Wynn, to Keep houses of entertainment at their places of Residence in this County.

Wednesday the 5th of June 1805   [155]

Ordered, that the Sum of Eight dollars & Seventy five Cents be paid to John Truman, in full for expenses on the Joal up to this date. Paid.

Wm Rabun
Stephen Evans
Richard A. Blount

Court Adjourned until Court in Course.

Ja^s Lewis, Clk

Monday July 29th 1805   [156]

Court Met.

Present, their Honors   William Rabun }
                                         Richard A. Blount } Esq^{rs}
                                         & John Crowder }

Ordered, that William Bridges, an Orphan child, be bound to Jonathan Clowers until he becomes of lawful Age.

Ordered, that Thomas Clayton, George Stewart & C°, W^m & James Lewis, & James H. Jones & C° have license to retail Spirituous liquors at their Places of residence in this County.

Ordered, that Duke Hamilton, Bird Ferrell, and Nathaniel Waller be appointed commissioners to view and lay out a road leading from Devereux's Mill the nearest and best way to Carr's on the Montpellier Road, and the following hands to work on the Same, (Viz.)

Ja^s Musselwhite, James

Monday July 29th 1805 [157]

Tomberlin, Widow Stell, Mrs Ann Kenan, Curtis Conway, Thomas Vickers, Cader Powell, Stephen Pearson, John Middlebrooks, Obadiah Lowe, Andrew Russell, James Johnson, Jacob Johnson, & that Thomas Vickers be Overseer of the same. issued.

Ordered, that Rutha Triplett, an Orphan child, be bound to Esom D. Franklin until she becomes of lawful age.

~~Ordered, that Rutha Triplett, an Orphan child~~

Ordered, that George, Edwin, Nancy Triplett, orphan children, be bound to James Montgomery until they become of lawful Age.

Ordered, that Samuel Harwell have License to retail Spirituous Liquors at his place of residence in this County. paid.

Ordered, that Shirley Sledge, Minns Sledge, & Dred Rogers be appointed Commissioners to view and lay out a road the nearest and best way from the Greene County line the nearest and best way to Jeremiah Thrower's ferry on the Oconee River.

Monday July 29th 1805 [158]

Ordered, that thirty dollars be and the same is hereby appropriated out of the County funds to Samuel Hall as his fees for Services rendered as Coroner. Paid.

Ordered, that the Sum of two hundred & forty dollars Seven & half Cents be & the same is hereby appropriated to John Truman, Esqr in full for Jail expenses for Sundry persons.

Ordered, that the Sum of fourteen dollars Eighty seven & half Cents be and the Same is hereby appropriated to James Lewis for providing Weights & Measures for the public use. Paid.

Ordered, that the road leading from Lindzey Robert's field to Dennis's Mill, from thence to intersect a road leading from Eilands Mill to a road leading to the rocklanding, & that said road be opened, not exceeding twelve feet. iss^d.

Ordered, that James Garey and John C. Slocomb be & they are hereby appointed Commissioners, to join any commissioners that may be appointed on the part of the County of Washington, to let to the lowest bidder the building of the bridge over Buffaloe at [blot] [faint] County line.

Monday July 29th 1805   [159]

Ordered, that the Sum of Six dollars fifty three & three fourth Cents be and the Same is hereby appropriated and paid to David Erwin in full for an Estray cow & yearling, after deducting the lawful fees.

Ordered, that Tisey Thomas & William Cureton be & they are hereby appointed Commissioners to join any commissioners that may be appointed on the part of Warren County to let to the lowest bidder the building a bridge over Ogeechee River at Co^l William Bird's Mill.

Ordered, that the following hands be subject to work on the road from the [smear] leading along by Joshua Claud's to Sparta, (Viz.)

Saml Hall, James Hall, [smear] & Taylor, Wm Sanford, Fred^k Sanford, Willie Abercrombie, Thos Foard, Saml Butts, Richd H. Carew, Philip Turner, Isaac Evans, Andrew Caldwell, Andrew Collins, Alex Martin, Joshua Claud, James Moss, Henry Moss, Mrs Pinkston, Henry Pinkston, Charles Abercrombie, John Abercrombie, Elisha King, Ja^s W. Jones, Ambrose Jones, Henry Darnell, Wm Lewis, Ja^s Lewis, Arch^d Martin, Edmond Evans, Jo^s Biggham, Stewart Anderson, Will Terrell, & Dennis L. Ryan, & that Joshua Claud be overseer of the same.

                           J̶n̶°̶ ̶C̶r̶o̶w̶d̶e̶r̶
W̶$̶^̶m̶$̶ ̶R̶a̶b̶u̶n̶   R̶i̶c̶h̶a̶r̶d̶ ̶B̶l̶o̶u̶n̶t̶

Monday the July 29th 1805 [160]

It appearing to the Court, that a citation for the sale of a lot of land lying in the town of Sparta, adjoining John Lucas, on broad Street, belonging to the Estate of John Mitchell, deceased, has been published in terms of the Act in such cases provided, it is Ordered, that the Administrators of the said John Mitchell, Deceased, do sell the said lot of land for the benefit of the heirs and creditors of said dec^d, agreeable to the terms of said Act.

Ordered, that the Sum of four dollars thirty one & one fourth Cents be appropriated & paid to Dennis L. Ryan for services rendered as Printer.

Jno Crowder
Wm Rabun
Richard Blount

Court adjourned until Court in Course.

Attest. Ja^s Lewis, Clk

Tuesday July the 30th 1805 [161]

Ordered, that the Sum of thirty dollars be and the same is hereby Appropriated and paid to Thomas Seale, as an indigent person. $5.00 paid.

Ordered, that the Sum of thirty dollars be and the same is hereby Appropriated and paid to Hannah Asberry, as an indigent person. paid.

[faint]
[faint]
Stephen Evans

Court adjourned until Court in Course.

Attest. Ja^s Lewis, Clk

Tuesday October the 1st 1805 [162]

Present, their Honors   William Rabun }
    Stephen Evans & } Esq^{rs}
    John Crowder   }

Ordered, that the Sum of two hundred and eighteen dollars & eighty two Cents be and the same is hereby appropriated & paid to Joseph Carter, Es^{qr}, in full for building a Bridge across Ogeechee at Lucas's Mill. paid.

Ordered, that Tavern license be granted to Reese & Beall, Jonathan Davis, James Waller, W^m & Thomas Hudson, William Sandford, Richard H. Carew, & Edmond Beard, to Keep houses of entertainment at their places of residence in this County.

Ordered, that the Sum of Eighty eight dollars & fifty Cents be appropriated & paid to John Freeman, Jaoler, for victualling & other services done Casey, Munroe, pare, & Massey, prisoners.

Tuesday October the 1st 1805   [163]

Ordered, that the sum of twelve dollars be appropriated & paid to James Hamilton, for services rendered as Sheriff. Paid.

Ordered, that the sum of six dollars & ninety five Cents be appropriated and paid Clements's Ben, for Ironing prisoners and repairing the Goal. Paid.

Ordered, that the sum of thirty two dollars thirty seven & half Cents be appropriated & paid to James Hall, as Sergeant of the Guard for conducting prisoners from Sparta to Wilkes Goal. Paid.

Ordered, that the sum of ten dollars be appropriated & paid to Stephen Clements, for Guarding Isaac Munroe & Barnaby Pare, prisoners to Augusta. Paid.

Ordered, that the sum of twenty dollars thirty Seven & half Cents be appropriated & Paid to Dennis L. Ryan, for services rendered as Printer.

Tuesday October the 1st 1805   [164]

Ordered, that the Sum of ten dollars be appropriated & paid to William Lewis, for services rendered as Guard. Paid.

Ordered, that the sum of Eight Dollars be appropriated & paid to Vines Harwell, for services rendered as Guard.

Ordered, that the sum of eleven dollars thirty six & half Cents be appropriated & paid to John Pryor, as constable for conducting Prisoners to Goal.

Ordered, that one Dollar each be appropriated and paid to Stephen Jones, Thos Parmer, William Hearn, Charles Butler, Levi Ellis, Francis Dansey, Henry Hammond, & Larkin Turner, for their Services in guarding the Jail in term of the Superior Court at August Term 1805.

Ordered, that John McLemore be & he is hereby appointed Overseer of the road leading from Mrs Tison's lane to Nathaniel Waller's, & the following hands subject to work thereon (Viz.)

Bird Ferrell, Mrs Tison, Nathaniel Waller, William Bazer, George & Newman Richardson, Francis Jeter, & Nathaniel Breedlove.

Ordered, that the Sum of three dollars be appropriated and paid to Hamlin Lewis for Services as Deputy Sheriff.

Tuesday October the 1st 1805   [165]

Ordered, that John Kilgore, Junr be & he is hereby appointed overseer of the road leading from Powelton to Samuel Shye's on the Sunbury Road, & on that part which lies between Powelton & Mitchell's Road, Dis^t N° 1, & the following hands work on the same, Viz.

Joseph Minton, Charles Oliver, Charles Sturdivant, Matthew Drake, William Kilgore, & Richard Shipp. iss^d.

Ordered, that John Spight be & he is hereby appointed overseer of the road leading from Mitchell's Road to Fulsom's Creek, Dis^t N° 2, & the following hands work thereon (Viz.)

John Kilgore, Senr, Charles Kilgore, Levi Spight, Matthew Rabun, William Rabun, Lewis Tanner, William Spight, William Hardwick, Barnaby Shivers, Willis Shivers, Benjamin Humphrey, John Godwizer, & William Battle. iss^d.

Ordered, that Abner Kelly be & he is hereby appointed overseer of the road leading from Fulsom's Creek to the George Town road, Dis^t N° 3, & the following hands to work thereon (Viz.)

Starling Savage, Eben^r Callaway, James Tilman, Th^o Mason John Hall, Wm Mason, Danl Dennis, John Kelly, Wm Seales, Danl Seales, Spencer Seales, Archibald Seals, & Wm Murphey, & Thomas Seales.

Tuesday the 1ˢᵗ October 1805 [166]

Ordered, that the Sum of one Dollar each be appropriated & paid to John Turner, Joseph Cooper, Thoˢ Foard, Bird Ferrell, John Chambers, Joseph B. Chambers (paid), William Bullock, Phillip Turner, Samuel Hall, for their Services in guarding the Jail in time of the Superior Court at August Term 1805.

Ordered, that the Sum of Six dollars be and the same is hereby appropriated & Paid to William Griggs, in full for Keeping William Clayton, an indigent person. paid.

          Wᵐ Rabun
          Jnº Crowder
          Stephen Evans

Attest. Jaˢ Lewis, Clk

Court adjourned until the last Monday in November.

       Chambers 2ⁿᵈ November 1805   [167]

Present, their Honors   Stephen Evans
             Richard Blount
             & John Crowder

Hamlin Lewis, Sheriff elect, came forward and was qualified agreeable to law.

          Richard Blount
          Stephen Evans
          Jnº Crowder

Attest. Alex Martin, pro Clk

         January the 6ᵗʰ 1806   [168]

Court met Pursuant to Adjournment.

Present, their Honors   John W. Devereux }
             William Rabun } Esqʳˢ
             Stephen Evans & }
             Richard A. Blount }

The Court and Justices of the peace attended & proceeded to the election of Receiver of Tax returns & Collector of Taxes for the present year, and on closing the polls, it appeared that John Comer, Esquire was duly elected Receiver of Tax Returns & Leonard Abercrombie, Esquire, Collector of Taxes.

Ordered, that Tavern license be granted ~~William~~ Joseph Carr, Hubert Reynolds & C°, Thomas Crowder & C°, Thomas Simmons, Sampson Duggar, & William Bivins, to retail Spirituous liquors at their respective places of residence in this County.

January the 6th 1806 [169]

Ordered, that John Brown & John Peace be and they are hereby appointed Constables in Captain Barksdale's District.

And Daniel Dennis for Capt Clark's District, also William Miles & Daniel Candler for Capt Candler's District. Also, that all other Constables who have served the year 1805 are hereby continued, & the several Justices also take bonds with sufficient security for their performance.

Ordered, that Tavern License be granted to Samuel M. Devereux & C° to retail spirituous liquors at their place of residence in the County.

Ordered, that John Daniel be & he is hereby appointed a Justice of the Peace in Capt Graybill's Dist, in place of Hubert Reynolds, resigned.

And Ephraim Whittington in Capt Slocomb's Dist, in place of Francis Trawick, resigned.

William Hudson in Capt Hudson's District, in place of Robert Holt, deceased.

January 6th 1806 [170]

And John Randle, in place of Frederick Tucker, deceased, Capt Connel's District.

Ordered, that the Sum of ten dollars be appropriated to ~~Henry~~ John Trippe, ten dollars to John Thweatt, ten dollars to Moses Wylie, Eight Dollars to John Hamilton, Eight Dollars to Wyatt Collier, Eight Dollars to Vines Harwell, Eight Dollars to Ambrose Jones, also two Dollars to ~~Henry~~ John Trippe, for expenses on prisoners & guarding them to Augusta, Viz. Isaac Monroe & Barnaby Parr. Paid.

Ordered, That Robert Hix Bonner and Alexander Bellamy be and they are hereby appointed Justices of the Peace in Capt Bass's District, in place of John Matthews and Peter Flournoy, removed out of the County.

Ordered, that one fifth of the Genl Tax be appropriated as a County Tax for the year 1805.

Ordered, that Tavern License be granted to Abraham Miles, William James, & Chapman & C° to retail Spirituous liquors at their places of residence in this County.

        Wm Rabun
        Jn° W. Devereux &
        Stephen Evans

Ja^s Lewis, Clk

At an Inferior Court (for County business) began and held in and for the [171] County of Hancock on Monday the third day of February 1806.

Present, their Honors   Stephen Evans }
              Jn° W. Devereux } Esquires
              John Crowder   }

Daniel Melson, George Smith, & Joseph Cooper, having been appointed to review the Road leading from Sparta to Cooper's Ferry on the Oconee River, Report that they find it necessary for said Road to be opened through Presley Ingram's field on the West Side of Fort Creek, where it was formerly laid out by consent of Stith Parham, who then owned the Land, and also through another field on the same direction, taking off only a very Small part, also through Daniel Melson's field by consent, also through Miles Graves' field by Consent.

It is therefore ordered, that the Overseer and the hands subject to work on said Road do Keep the same in repair to the Ferry, and that Lewis Sanders be added to the hands Subject to work thereon.

        February the 3rd 1806   [172]

Ordered, that the Clerk do issue to Willie Abercrombie License to retail Spirituous liquors by the small at his Store, known by the name of Mount Hope, to bear date from the 28th of October last.

Ordered, that the sum of fourteen dollars be appropriated to the use of John Brown for boarding William Kelley & four in family seven days, they being parishioners, and that the Clerk pay the same in Order. Paid.

Ordered, that Tavern License be granted to Jameson Anders, Richard Waller, John Freeman, Shearwood Wommack, & Edward Clanton to retail Spirituous liquors at their places of residence in this County.

Ordered, that Joseph Carr, Davis Felps, & Hicks Bonner be and they are hereby appointed Commissioners to lay out a Road from Joseph Carr's to William Sheffield's Ferry on the Oconee River, opposite the mouth of Little River, the nearest and most convenient way, and that Charles Miller be appointed Overseer to open and Keep the same in repair.

February the 3rd 1806 [173]

Ordered, That the following hands be subject to work on the road leading from Baxter's Mills on Shoulderbone to the Oconee River, to wit.

Edward Clanton, James Farley, Elizabeth Sledges, Chappel Sledge, John Sledges, Philemon Foster, Levi Foster, Benjamin Anderson, Daniel Lewis, Stephen Evans, Samuel Dent, Greene Wynne, John Low, Burton Sanders, Daniel Sanders, Thomas Wagnon, & Thomas Heath, & that John Sledge be appointed Overseer of the Same in the place of Daniel Wagnon.

Ordered, That James Askey be appointed Overseer in the place of Edmond Butler, dec^d. And that the ~~following~~ hands belonging to the following persons be Subject to work thereon, to wit.

Bennit Hilsman, Henry Byrom, James Byrom, Francis Butler, Josiah Askey, Robert Bryan, Henry Lucas, Edmond Garrett, & Mourning Garrett.

Ordered, That William Devereux, Francis Smith, Isaiah Eiland, and William Bivins be and they are hereby appointed Commissioners to lay out a road from Elijah Lingo's Mill on Town Creek to Candler's bend on the Oconee River, opposite Milledgeville. And that the hands belonging to the following persons & person be Subject to work thereon, to wit.

Elijah Lingo, John Jones, Peleg Rogers, John Bivins, Shadrack Bivins, James Ryley, Esom Franklin, William Bivins, Philip Levar, Isaiah Eiland, John

Murphey, John Conner, Dempsy Austin, Francis Smith, Ja^s Montgomery, Wm Warden, Hiram Baldwin, Thomas Cavannah,

February the 3rd 1806 [174]

Edward Cavannah, George Cavanah, Thomas Miles, Isaac Hall, & [blank] Dryless, And that Phillip Levar be appointed overseer to open & Keep the same in repair.

Ordered, that John Henderson be appointed Guardian to Christopher and James Harrison, Orphans of Pleasant Harrison, in the place of Robert Simms.

Ordered, that Nathan Nolley, Simon Harris, & John Harris be bound to Thomas Lancaster, to learn the Taylor's trade, until they arrive to the age of twenty one years of Age.

Ordered, that Tavern Licence be granted to George Gray, to retail spirits at his House.

Ordered, That the sum of one hundred dollars be appropriated to and for the use of William Kelly & family, Parishioners, And the same be paid into the hands of the Overseers of the Poor in order.

Ordered, That Wingate Hall be appointed a Justice of the Peace in Capt Candler's District.

Ordered, That Robert Simms be appointed a Justice of the Peace in Capt Connell's District.

Ordered, That Samuel Dent be appointed a Justice of the Peace in Capt Huff's District.

February the 3rd 1806 [175]

Ordered, That Thomas J. Slatter be appointed a Justice of the Peace in Capt Holt's Dis^t.

Ordered, That the Sum of twenty five dollars & twenty five Cents be appropriated and paid to John Freeman, Esqr, in full for the Jail Expenses of Joseph B. Jones, Also two dollars & fifty Cents to Hamlin Lewis, D. Sheriff, Also two dollars & fifty Cents to the Clerk of the Inferior Court.

Court then Adjourned until the Tuesday after the first Monday in March.

$$\text{Jn}^\text{o}\text{ W. Devereux}$$
$$\text{Jn}^\text{o}\text{ Crowder}$$
$$\text{Stephen Evans}$$

Test. Ja^s Lewis, Clk

Monday the 7th of April 1806   [176]

Court met pursuant to adjournment.

Present, their Honors   William Rabun }
                                       Stephen Evans } Esquires
                                       John Crowder }
                                       John W. Devereux }
                                       & Richard Blount }

Ordered, that James Bridges, an Orphan Child, be bound to William Barber until he becomes of lawful age. borp^t.

Ordered, that the Sum of forty dollars be appropriated and paid to Joab Durham for Keeping William Clark, a Parishioner for the year 1805. Paid.

Ordered, that Tavern License be granted to Thweatt & Greene to retail Spirituous liquors at their place of residence in this County to bear date from the 10th of March. 8.00

Ordered, that Tavern License be granted to Henry Brown, [faint] & John C. Currie to retail Spirituous liquor at their places of residences in this County.

Ordered, that the Sum of three dollars each to James Hamilton and Six Men for one day, also the Sum of three dollars each to James Hamilton & five men for three days & a half for Guarding prisoners to Wilkes Jail. Paid.

Monday the 7th of April 1806   [177]

Ordered, That the Sum of One hundred & Sixty Eight dollars be appropriated and paid to William Ray, being the proportionable part of Hancock County for building a Bridge across Buffaloe Creek at the dividing line Between Hancock & Washington Counties. P^d.

Ordered, that the following hands be subject to work on the Road from the old County line to the fork below Edmond Beard's (Viz.)

Benj^a Thompson, Martin Armstrong, Joseph Hartley, Young Goodwin, James Walker, Reuben Walker, Thomas Lovet, Nathan Harris, James Shye, Simon Shye, Isham Huckaby, Isaac Blackshear, & Davis Smith, Overseer of the Same.

Ordered, that the following hands be subject to work on the road leading from Edmond Beard's to Little Ogeechee (Viz.)

Francis Lewis, Senr, Richard Blount, James Wood, Thomas Griffin, Joseph Kelley, [blank] Hughbanks, John Dickson, Benj^a Dickson, Richard Taylor, Danl John, Samuel John, Solomon Phillips, David Huckaby, George Fagan, Thomas Fagan, & James Page, Overseer.

Ordered, That the sum of ten dollars be appropriated and paid to Young Goodwin for Keeping William Clark. paid.

Ordered, that the Sum of thirty dollars be appropriated and paid to George Miller for Keeping Edward Miller, a Parishioner for the year 1806. p^d in full.

Monday the 7th of April 1806   [178]

Ordered, that John & Spias Hennon, Orphans of James Hennon, be bound to John Tillmon, until they become of lawful Age.

Ordered, the Sum of thirty dollars be appropriated to ~~John~~ [blot] Edith Williams for Keeping William Clark, a Parishioner, until the first Monday in January next. paid.

Ordered, That the sum of ten dollars Sixty Eight & three quarter Cents be appropriated and paid to Dennis L. Ryan, for services as printer.

Ordered, that Isaiah ~~Eiland~~ Parker be allowed the Sum of thirty dollars for an illegitimate Child of Susannah Sturdivant's, left in her hands at the age of three weeks for six months, & that the said Isaiah Parker giving bond and security for the further maintenance of said infant free from County expense, until the said infant arrives to lawful Age.

Ordered, that the following hands be subject to work on the road from Bivins's to Montpellier & Abraham Miles be Overseer of the same (viz.)

Monday the 7th of April 1806 [179]

Stewart Peace, Wm Allain, Allen Greene, Simon Rogers, Wm Baldwin, Mr Dubois, Alex^r Greene, Wm Allen, Henry Darnell, Thompson Bird, Wm James, A. Miles, George Sampson, Isaiah Chapman, Dennis Doyle, Daniel McRay, Benj^a Moreland, M^rs McK[smear], Jesse Ellis, Jeremiah Miles, Wm Miles, Ransom Lea, Saml Slaughter, Dubois Champion, David Parker, Neill Ferguson, Jonathan Colbert, Widow Rogers, Dempsy Justice, Thomas Callaway, Thomas Hadaway, Henry Jones, Micajah Middlebrooks, John Moran, Saml Kilpatrick, Wilson Brown, Jesse Talbert, & Thomas Talbert. iss^d.

Ordered, that an Order made 6th June 1803, a Road from Holt's Mill to Salem be the same is hereby established, & the following hands work thereon (Viz.)

Saml Slaughter, Dubois Chapman, David Parker, Ransom Lea, Wm Miles, Hill Chapman, Jesse Ellis, Ja^s Montgomery, John Brown, James Dubois, & David Parker, Overseer of the same.

Ordered, that the Sum of twenty five dollars be appropriated to the use of Mrs Hendriken for boarding & Clothing Thomas Vaughan. Paid.

Monday the 7th of April 1806 [180]

Ordered, That a road be laid out near Mark Gonder's store, leading the most direct way to William Shivers's Mill, & from thence with the Road leading from the piney woods house to Jonas Shivers' at Jesse Pope's fence, & that Mark Gonder, Samuel Barron, & Barnaby Shivers be appointed Commissioners to lay out the same, And the following hands work thereon (Viz.)

Saml Barron, Saml Pope, Abner Atkinson, Willis Shivers, Barnaby Shivers, Mary Lockhart, Mark Gonder, Sterling Savage, & Barnaby Shivers, Overseer of the same.

Ordered, That Thaddeus Holt be and he is hereby Authorized to cut down the bank of the river at the Western end of Union Street in the Town of Montpellier on the Oconee River and make use of the same for one year.

Ordered, that a road be laid out from John C. Currie's, most direct and convenient way to James Barron's ferry on the Oconee river, that John Lamar, John Humphries, Zachariah Booth be and they are hereby Appointed Commissioners to lay out the same, & that George Thompson be Overseer of the same.

Monday the 7th of April 1806 [181]

Jeremiah Mathews, John Lamar, John Simons, Richard Gra[smear], George Thompson, [smear] Humphries, Zachariah Booth, Willis Bellerson, Obadiah Morris, James Barron, Abner Abercrombie do work thereon.

Ordered, that the following persons be authorized to Establish Public Ferrys on the Eastern bank of the Oconee River in this County.

To Ignatius Few, on the road leading from Barns' to his landing.

To James Barrows, on the road lading from Boothe's Mount to his landing.

To Hardy Cain's, on the road leading from Sparta to his landing.

To Peter Mahone's, on the road leading from Sparta to his landing.

To Joseph Cooper, on the road leading from Sparta to his landing.

To James Yarbrough, on the road leading from Sparta to his landing.

And that the following be the rates of ferriage.

For a four wheel carriage fifty Cents, for two wheel D° twenty five Cents, for man & horse twelve & half Cents, for a foot passage Six & ¼ Cents, Cattle 4 Cts, Hogs, Sheep, & Goats 2 Cents.

Monday the 7th of April 1806 [182]

Ordered, that the sum of [blot] Seventy five dollars be appropriated in favor of James Thomas, for Boading & Clothing Patsey Martin, until the 1st Monday in January next. And that the sum of five dollars be appropriated and paid to the Widow Smith. Paid.

         Jn° Crowder
         Jn° W. Devereux
         Richard Blount

Court Adjourned until 1st Monday in May.

Attest. Ja's Lewis, Clk

Monday May the 5th 1806 [183]

Court met pursuant to adjournment.

Present, their Honors   William Rabun   }
                          John Crowder   } Esquires
                          Stephen Evans & }
                          Richard A. Blount }

Ordered, That John Rivers be and he is hereby appointed a Justice of the Peace in Capt Weekes's District, in place of John Comer, removed. iss^d.

Ordered, that the Sum of forty two Dollars seventy five cents be appropriated & paid to Lewis Goodwyn, being the proportionable part of Hancock County for building a Bridge across Ogeechee at Bird's Mills. paid.

Ordered, That Tavern Licence be granted to Philip Turner to retail Spirituous liquors at his place of residence in Sparta for one year.

Ordered, that a Ferry be Established on the East side of the Oconee at Abraham Borland's landing & that a road be laid out the nearest and best way from said landing to John Humphries' and that John Bivins, [blot] Starling Bass, Thomas Morris be

Monday May the 5th 1806 [184]

and they are hereby appointed Commissioners for the same and report thereon to this Court. iss^d.

Ordered, That a road be laid out the nearest and best way from Reynolds's Store on Island Creek to the ford on Rocky Creek, where the Cedar Shoal road crosses the same, & that Herbert Reynolds, Allen Thompson, & John Johnson be & they are hereby appointed Commissioners for the same, & make a report thereon to the Court. Iss^d.

Ordered, That Jacob Gunn be and he is hereby appointed Overseer of the road leading from the flower fork of Derrisa's Creek to Rocky Creek, & the following hands work thereon, Viz.

Andrew Borland, Peter Freeny, James Boswell, John Peterson, Abraham Borland, James Barrow, & Zachariah Boothe.

Ordered, that a Ferry be established on the East side of the Oconee opposite the mouth of little River, at William Shuffield's landing.

Eli Harris & C° }
    vs   } Attachment
Mark Moore }

The above Tachment have

Monday May the 5th 1806   [185]

been levied upon Carpenter's tools, Blacksmith's Tools, Corn, & fodder, which are of a perishable nature.

Ordered, that the said Articles of property so levied upon as aforesaid be by the Sheriff of this County sold at Eli Harris & C°'s Store at Dane Hill, after giving ten days public notice at that place and at the Court House of said County, and that the monies arising from said Sale be by the Sheriff deposited in the Clerk's Office of said Court to be subject to the further Order of Court in said Case.

Ordered, that Tavern Licence be granted to Mark Gonder & C° to retail spirituous liquors at their places of residence in this County. paid.

Ordered, that Tavern Licence be granted to Willis Shivers to retail spirituous liquors at his place of residence in this County & also for Capt Samuel Hall. paid.

Monday May the 5th 1806   [186]

Ordered, that Samuel Barron be appointed Overseer of the road leading from Major Evans's to Fulsom's Creek, & the following hands work thereon (Viz.)

Mark Gonder, Wm Chandler, Jas Wilson, George Larey, Jonathan Davis, Wm Gay, Saml Watts, Thos Gay, Saml Pope, Starling Savage, George Allen, & Joseph Deloach. issd.

Ordered, That ~~Commissioners~~ Edward Clanton, Minns Sledge, Robert Clark, William Clark, & Dread Rogers be appointed commissioners to lay out a road from the Greene County line by Bunker's Hill to Clanton's ferry on the Oconee River.

$\qquad\qquad\qquad\qquad$ Wm Rabun
$\qquad\qquad\qquad\qquad$ Richard Blount
$\qquad\qquad\qquad\qquad$ Jno Crowder
$\qquad\qquad\qquad\qquad$ Stephen Evans

Court Adjourned until Court in Course.

Attest. Ja^s Lewis, Clk

$\qquad\qquad\qquad$ Wednesday June the 4th 1806 $\qquad\qquad$ [187]

Court met.

Present, their Honors $\qquad\qquad$ Stephen Evans }
$\qquad\qquad\qquad\qquad\qquad\qquad$ John Crowder & } Esquires
$\qquad\qquad\qquad\qquad\qquad\qquad$ Richard A. Blount }

Ordered, That the Sum of forty one dollars be paid out of the County funds to John F. Flournoy for repairing the Bridge over Ogeechee at Mitchell's Mill. paid.

Ordered, That Tavern License be granted to Dennis Doyle & Birdsong & Lattimer to retail spirituous liquors at their places of residence in this County.

Ordered, That Hartwell Garey be & he is hereby appointed a Justice of the peace, in place of William Gilliland, resigned, in Capt Barksdale's District.

$\qquad\qquad\qquad\qquad$ Richard Blount
$\qquad\qquad\qquad\qquad$ Jno Crowder
$\qquad\qquad\qquad\qquad$ Stephen Evans

Court Adjourned until Court in Course.

Test. Ja^s Lewis, Clk

Monday July the 7th 1806 [188]

Court met pursuant to adjournment.

Present, their Honors   William Rabun }
            Stephen Evans } Esq^{rs}
            Richard A. Blount }
            John Crowder }

Ordered, That the following hands be subject to work on the Road leading from Abraham Borland's ferry to John Humphries's, Viz.

Zachariah Boothe, Thomas Morris, & that Abraham Borland be and he is hereby appointed Overseer of the same. Iss^d.

Ordered, That Tavern Licence be granted to Benjamin J. Harper to retail spirituous liquors at his place of residence in this County. paid.

Ordered, That Tavern licence be granted to John Burch to retail spirituous liquors at his place of residence in this County.

Monday July the 7th 1806 [189]

Ordered, That a ferry be established on the east Side of the Oconee River at Phillip Catching's landing, & that Benjamin Parker, Jeremiah Bonner, & Elisha Moran be and they are hereby appointed Commissioners to view and lay out a Road the nearest and best way from Bonner's Mill on Town Creek to said ferry.

Ordered, That John Turner, William Gilliland, and Greenberry Pinkston be and they are hereby appointed commissioners to view and lay out a Road the nearest and best way from Sparta to the forks of this Road, where Benjamin Averett formerly lived (Viz.) from Sparta by John Pinkston's and William Gilliland's.

            Wm Rabun
            Jno Crowder
            Richard Blount
            Stephen Evans

Court Adjourned until Court in Course.

Ja^s Lewis, Clk

Monday July the 7th 1806 [190]

In conformity to an act of the Gen¹ Assembly for the distribution of lands lately ceded by the Creek Indians, the following persons were appointed to take list of persons names entitled to land in the lottery for the County of Hancock, To wit.

William Rabun for Maj^r Davis's Battalion, Stephen Evans for Maj^r Cauley's d°, Richard Blount for Maj^r Taliaferro's d°, John Crowder for Maj^r Reid's d°.

Test. Ja^s Lewis, Clk

Monday September the 1st 1806 [191]

Court met pursuant to adjournment.

Present, their Honors   William Rabun   }
                                     Richard A. Blount } Esq^{rs}
                                     & John Crowder   }

Ordered, That the following hands be and they are hereby Subject to work on the Road leading from the fork at William H. Matthews' to the road leading from James Halliday's (Viz.)

Benjamin Leonard, John Leonard, Jeremiah Worsham, James Jernigan, Wm Alford, Senr, Wm Alford, Junr, Owen Alford, Joseph Cooper, Nicholas Darby, & Benjamin Leonard Overseer of the Same.

Francis Bigham and Joseph Bigham having presented their Petitions for naturalization and Subscribed the following Oath.

It is Ordered, that they be Citizens of the United States and they be entitled to all the benefits, priviledges, and unnuities, which any fell bow Citizen of the United States are entitled to.

Monday September the 1st 1806 [192]

I, Francis Bigham, do solemnly swear that I will support the Constitution of the United States, that I will renounce all allegeince to every other prince, Power,

Potentate, or sovereign whatsoever, particularly to that of George the third, King of Great Britain, to whom I was before a Subject. So help me God.

Fra^s Biggam

I, Joseph Biggam, do solemnly swear that I will support the Constitution of the United States, that I will renounce all allegience to every other prince, Power, Potentate, or sovereign whatsoever, particularly to that of George the third, King of Great Britain, to whom I was before a Subject. So help me God.

Joseph Biggam

Ordered, that the following hands be subject to work on the Road leading from Shadrack Rees to main fork Creek at Trippe's old place, and the following hands work thereon (Viz.)

Saml White, Turner Hunt, Mason Harwell, Saml Cowles, Francis Ross, Saml Harris, Absolom Harris, Ed^m Oneal, John Bass, Wm Hargrove, Archibald Turner, Saml Turner, John White, Enoch Wallen, Reuben Herndon, & Henry Turner Overseer of the same.

Monday September the 1st 1806   [193]

Ordered, That Henry Colquitt have leave to turn the Road leading from Sparta to Greensborough, beginning at or near Co^l Lucas's Corner tree Standing on the road, and run a direct line so as to leave Taylor Nelson's Corner tree on the left hand of the road, and thence into the old road at the corner of said Nelson's fence.

Ordered, That Tavern Licence be granted Halliday & Burch, Reese & Bealle, Wilson Brown, W^m & Ja^s Lewis to retail spirituous liquors at their places of residence in this County for one year.

Ordered, That Nathan Breedlove be and he is hereby appointed overseer of the road leading from Baxter's Mill Road near Sparta to Mrs Tyson's lane, & the former hands work thereon. iss^d.

Ordered, That Newman Richardson be & he is hereby appointed Overseer of the road leading from Mrs Tyson's lane to Nathaniel Waller, Esqr, & the former hands work thereon. iss^d.

Ordered, That Samuel M. Devereux be & he is hereby appointed Overseer of the road leading from Nathaniel Waller's to Charles McDonald's, & the former hands work thereon. iss^d.

Ordered, that Elisha Harris be and he is hereby appointed Overseer of the road leading from Saml M. Devereux's Store to Town Creek near [faint], & the former hands work thereon.

Monday September the 1st 1806   [194]

Ordered, That Dempsey Justice, Deberry Chapman, James Debose, John Montgomery, and Samuel Slaughter be appointed to assess the damage Occasioned by the public road leading through Jesse Talbert's plantation, from Holt's Mills to Salem, and make report under their hands to the next Inferior Court. iss^d.

Ordered, that Minn McGaughey be Overseer of the road leading from Sparta by Obadiah Richardson's, & from said Richardson's to the Creek called Shoulderbone at Doctor Lane's, & the following hands work thereon, Viz.

O. Richardson, Simon Holt, Senr, Gibble Thomas, Evan Long, John Thomas, Lem^l Barnes, E. Marchman, S. Marchman, John Bishop, Jesse Maddox, Planner Shoars, Widow Thomas, Abel Barnes, Nathan Barnes, Wm Bullock, Benj^a Williams, Wm Horton, Moulford Lawson.

Ordered, That the Sum of eight dollars & seventy five Cents be appropriated and paid to Hamlin Lewis, Sheriff, in full for executing Nathaniel Tait & finding rope.

Monday September the 1st 1806   [195]

Ordered, That Thomas Lawson be & he is hereby appointed overseer of the road leading from Obadiah Richardson's to Mr Mapp's on the Greensborough Road from Doctor Lane's, And the following hands work thereon, Viz.

Dudley Lawson, David Lawson, Robert Alston, Hamilton Bonner, Joseph Higgenbotham, Doct^r J. Lane, Wm Reese, Sol Bealle, Ed Broadnax, & John Lewis. iss^d.

Ordered, That Henry Dixon be & he is hereby appointed overseer of the road leading from O. Richardson's to the piney woods house, & the following hands work thereon (Viz.)

Isaac Adams, Saml Parsons, Ryley Marchman, Joseph Turner, Henry Dixon, John Caswell, James Waller, Wm Waller, Else Boyce, Gab^l Richardson, Henry Champion, David Carter, Abraham Carter, Lewis Tyus, Nathan Culver, Lewis Bandy. iss^d.

Ordered, That the Sum of five Dollars be appropriated and paid to Edmond Evans, in full for a coffin furnished Nathan Tait.

Ordered, that the Sum of Six dollars be & the same is hereby appropriated & paid to James Hamilton & Drury Reese, Six Dollars to Moses Wyley, Six Dollars to William Stanton, Six Dollars to Mark Armstrong p^d, in full for gurding Joseph Simms, a prisoner to Saundersville Jail, Viz. ~~Joseph~~

Monday September the 1st 1806 [196]

Ordered, That the Sum of twelve dollars & fifty Cents be appropriated & paid to Hannah Asberry, as an indigent person up to the 1st January 1807. paid.

        Wm Rabun
        Jno Crowder
        R. Blount

Court Adjourned until 1st Monday in ~~November~~ Dec^r.

Attest. Ja^s Lewis, Clk

Monday December the 1st 1806

Court met Pursuant to Adjournment.

Present, their Honors   William Rabun   }
             Stephen Evans   } Esquires
             Richard A. Blount }
             & John Crowder }

Ordered, That Tavern Licence be granted to Philip L. Simms to retail Spirituous liquors at his place of residence in Sparta.

Monday December the 1st 1806 [197]

Whereas, an Attachment in favor of John Manly was levied upon three Horses, Waggon, and gun, the property of Edward Davis, and the same being of a perishable nature.

It is Ordered, that the Sheriff of Hancock County do sell the said property in Sparta after giving ten days notice of the day of sale, and to deposit the monies arising from the same in the hands of the Clerk of the Inferior Court of said County to be Subject to the further Order of Court.

Ordered, that Tavern Licence be granted to William Sanford, Ichabud Thompson, William & Thomas Hudson, Mitchell & Jones to retail spirituous liquors at their places of residence in this County for one year.

Ordered, that Willie Abercrombie be & he is hereby appointed Overseer of the road leading from Fort Creek, near Nathan Sanders's to Log dam Creek. iss^d.

Ordered, that James Barnes be and he is hereby appointed overseer of the road leading from Asa Alexander's to Hudsons' Mill, in place of Levi Daniel. Also Absalom Barnes in place of Nathan Daniel on the road leading from Hudsons' Mill to Capt Bishop's on Beaverdam.

Monday December the 1st 1806 [198]

Ordered, that Lucy, a free girl of Coulour, be bound to Elizabeth Rogers, until she becomes of Lawful Age.

Ordered, that Matthew Averete be & he is hereby appointed Overseer of the Road from George Town to [blank] Linebe's, & the following hands work thereon (Viz.)

Thos Dixon, John Dixon, John Averet, Archelus Averete, Jeremiah Averete, David Averete, Matthew Averete, John Shoulders, David Shoulders, Ed Shoulders, Burwell Rachels, Ge^o Rachels, Wm Rachels, Thomas Pritchett, Nehemiah Smith, Wm Holliman, Eph^m Curtis, Thadeus Whittenton, Isaac Rosser, Jno Bryant, Wm Pritchett, Abraham Smith, West Vinson, Jno Battle, Zach^a Beckam, Robt Stripling.

Ordered, that Levin Moore be and he is hereby appointed Overseer of the Road leading from Bonner's Mill to Levin Moore's Still House on Derrisa's Creek & the following hands work thereon (Viz.)

Jn° Parker, Tho⁵ Hagans, Benjᵃ Parker, Jn° King, Elijah King, Arthur Danielly, George Miflin, M. Whitly Moore, Jacob Moore, Wᵐ Freeman, Joseph Freeman, Richᵈ Jordan, Obadiah Morris, Jeremiah Morris, Wᵐ Astin, Mathew Watkins, Smith Watson, Benjᵃ Parker.

Monday December the 1ˢᵗ 1806   [199]

Ordered, that the Sum of twelve dollars seventy five cents be appropriated & paid to Dennis L. Ryan, for services rendered the County for printing.

Ordered, that the Sum of forty five dollars forty seven & an half Cents be appropriated & paid to Jesse Talbert for damages done in running a public road through said Talbert's Plantation Agreeable to report of Commissioners. paid.

Ordered, that John Harbirt, William Dismuks, & Alexander Bellamy be appointed Commissioners to view & lay out a road, as petitioned by Joseph Carr, Senʳ, & report to the next Court.

Ordered, that Joseph Carr, Senʳ be appointed Overseer of the road from Carr's ferry to Chaˢ McDonald's, & the former hands work thereon.

Ordered, that Harris Horn be appointed Overseer of the Road leading from the ford at Island Creek to [smear] Boothe Mount, & the former hands work thereon.

Ordered, that John Butts (with the former hands) be appointed Overseer of a road leading from Joseph Car's to Mahone's ferry.

Ordered, that the Sum of fifty dollars be appropriated & paid to James Lewis, Clerk of the Inferior Court, for Stationary & Extra services in that capacity.

Monday December the 1st 1806 [200]

Ordered, that an Extra Tax of one third of the Genl Tax of said County be levied & Collected for the [blot] present year.

>   Richard Blount
>   Jno Crowder
>   Stephen Evans
>   Wm Rabun

Court Adjourned until Court in Course.

Ja^s Lewis, Clk

Hancock Inferior Court January 5th 1807

Present, their Honors   William Rabun }
                         Stephen Evans }
                         John Crowder   } Esq^{rs}
                         Richard A. Blount }
                         Bolling Hall   }

Monday January the 5th 1807 [201]

Ordered, that Tavern License be granted to William Bivins, Isaac Motley, Robert B. Glenn, & John Brown to retail spirituous liquors at their places of residence in Hancock County.

Ordered, that Tavern License be granted to Thomas Crowder & Co to retail Spirituous liquors at his place of residence in Powelton for one year. paid.

Ordered, that Tavern License be granted to Sampson Duggar to retail Spirituous liquors at his place of residence in Powelton.

Ordered, that Tavern License be granted John Abercrombie to retail Spirituous liquors at place of residence in Sparta.

The Court and Justices of the Peace Attended & proceeded to the election of a Receiver of Tax Returns and Collector of Taxes for the present year, and on closing the Polls, it appeared that James Hamilton was duly elected Receiver of Tax Returns, & Anderson Abercrombie, Esqr was duly elected Collector of Taxes.

Monday January the 5th 1807 [202]

Ordered, that Francis Jeter be & he is hereby Appointed a Constable for Capt Winslett's Dist.

And Wright Hill for Capt Birdsong's Do.

And John Dudley for Capt Harris's Do.

And Capt Hudson's Do.

Ordered, that Tavern Licence be granted to William James to retail Spirituous liquors at place of residence in Hancock County for one year.

Ordered, that Tavern Licence be granted to Thomas Simmons to retail Spirituous liquors at his place of residence in Powelton.

Ordered, that the Sum of fifteen dollars Quarterly be appropriated & Paid to the Widow Huchity, for the Space of one year, for the Support of two Bastard Children of Betsey Goodson, decd. Paid.

Ordered, that the Sum of thirty dollars be appropriated & paid to Nathan Asberry for Keeping Hannah Asberry till 1st ~~January~~ Saturday in October next. paid.

Also, thirty dollars to Edith Williams for Keeping William Clark. paid.

Also, thirty dollars to William Thomason for Keeping Richard Thomason. paid.

Also, forty dollars to George Linch for

Monday January the 5th 1807 [203]

Keeping Jesse Shivers.

Also, thirty dollars to James Wilkins for Keeping John Lee, all up to the first saturday in October Next.

Ordered, that Charles Miller be & he is hereby appointed Constable for Capt Smith's Dist.

Micajah Middlebrooks for Capt Kandler's Do.

Arthur Youngblood for Capt Holt's D^o.

Harris Horn for Capt Green's D^o.

John Peace for Capt Turner's D^o.

& Daniel Melson for Capt Waters's D^o.

And that the constables who are acting in the other districts in the County be & they are hereby Continued.

Ordered, that Richard B. Fletcher be & he is hereby appointed a Justice of the Peace in Capt Coffee's Dis^t, in place of Benjamin Whitfield, resigned.

And that William Hardwick be appointed a Justice of the Peace in Capt Shivers' Dis^t, in place of William Battle, resigned.

Ordered, that Aron Smith be appointed a Justice of the Peace in Capt Justice's

Monday January the 5th 1807

District, in place of Robert Hix Bonner, dec^d.

Ordered, that Isaiah Eilands be & he is hereby appointed Overseer of the Road leading from Lingo's Mill to Kandler's bend on the Oconee, & the following hands work thereon, Viz.

Elijah Lingo, Thos Callaway, [blank] Melson, Esom Franklin, Wm Bivins, Wm Beard, Jno Murphey, Jno Conner, Dempsey Justice, Francis Smith, A. Miles, Ja^s Montgomery, Wm Warden, Jacob Gimble, Wm Devereux's hands, Ja^s Works, Ge^o Miflin & Son, Davis & William Burge. iss^d.

Ordered, that the Sum of thirty dollars be Appropriated & paid for the Support of Thomas Campbell, till the first of October next. p^d $15.00

Ordered, that William Barnes be & he is hereby appointed a Justice of the Peace in Capt Barnes' District, in place of Duke Hamilton, Esqr, resigned.

Monday January the 5th 1807 [205]

Ordered, that Francis Lewis be & he is hereby appointed Overseer of the Road leading from the Green County line to Baxter's Mills, & the following hands work thereon, Viz.

James Wooten, David Wommack, Green Cato, Benjamin Parrot, Stith Evans, Abner Evans, William Walker, David Walker, John Hearn, Henry Forgerson, Joseph Middlebrooks, Thomas Middlebrooks, James Shackleford, Robert Adams, William Mills, William Adams, David Adams, Walter Hammilton, Chappel Heath, Robert Gilmore, Nathaniel Mathews, John Thomas, Stephen Wright, David Henry, Beachum Owens, Thomas Walker, Byren Shells, Hamlin Cook, John McNabb.

Ordered, that Benjamin Chappel be & he is hereby appointed Overseer of the road leading from Baxter's Mill to Clanton's ferry, & the following hands work thereon (Viz.)

Green Wynn, Saml Dent, Danl Low, Th^o Jones, John Williams, Ge^o Strawder, Burton Saunders, Daniel [faint], John Low, John Low, Senr, Benjamin Anderson, Alexander B[faint], Ephraim Rogers, Thos Heath, Philemon Foster, Levi Foster, [faint] Foster, John Foster, Junr, Hezekiah Singleton, Martha Sledge, Chappel Sledge, Turner Moreland, Edwd Clanton, James Farley, Dolly Chappel, [faint] John Chappel.

Court Adjourned till Thurday the 8th Jany 1807.

Ja^s Lewis, Clk

Thursday January 8th 1807 [206]

Court met agreeable to Adjournment.

Present, their Honors   Stephen Evans   }
                              Richard A. Blount } Esq^{rs}
                              & Bolling Hall   }

James Thomas, having made a satisfactory proof to this Court that a certain cow & calf sold by Hugh M. Comer, Esquire as an Estray is his right & property.

It is Ordered, that the Sum of Six dollars sixty seven & quarter cents be appropriated & paid to said Thomas in full for said Estray. paid.

Ordered, that Tavern License be granted to Isaac Hall & C° to retail Spirituous liquors at their place of residence in this County for one year.

Thursday the 8th of January 1807 [207]

It appearing to the Court that nine months public notice hath been given that application would be made to the Honorable the Inferior Court Court of Hancock County for leave to sell the one half of a tract of Land, containing One hundred & twenty Acres, lying & being in the County of Hancock on Buffaloe Creek, adjoining Isaac Dennis and others, being a part of the real estate of John Lewis, J^r, Dec^d, no person appearing to gainsay the said application.

It is Ordered, That the Administrators of the said John Lewis, J^r, Dec^d do sell the aforesaid tract of land after advertising the same in one of the public Gazettes of this State and at the Court House door of this County at least sixty days previous to the day of sale.

On the Petition of a number of persons praying that a road be opened from Thomas Rivers' leading by Samuel Hawkins to Frederick Lipham's.

It is Ordered, that Thomas Rivers, Samuel Hawkins, & Malone Mullins be & they are hereby appointed Commissioners to review the ground on which the Road prayed for is contemplated to be run, that they report the utility thereof

Thursday January the 8th 1807 [208]

to the next Inferior Court, together with the objections (if any made by persons through whose lands it is intended to be opened) together with a list of hands sufficiable to work thereon.

Ordered, that Frederick Lipham have the liberty of keeping a public ferry at his land on the Oconee River for one year, agreeable to the rates established heretofore.

Ordered, that James Harvey, Ichabud Thompson, Jeffrey Barksdale, Edward Butler, John Stephens be & they are hereby appointed Commissioners to review and make report to the next Court of the alteration necessary in the Road leading from Logdam Creek to Yarbrough's ferry, together with the hands liable to work thereon.

                                        Stephen Evans
                                        Richard Blount
                                        Bolling Hall

Court Adjourned until the 1st Monday February.

Jas Lewis, Clk

                    Tuesday January the 27th 1807   [209]

Present, their Honors   William Rabun }
                                              John Crowder & } Esqrs
                                              Bolling Hall   }

Russel Shorter }
     vs   }
Joseph Cooper }

On the Petition of Joseph Cooper, Sen Stating that he is confined in the common Jail of the County at the instance of Russel Shorter on a cassia as [illegible] & praying the benefit of the Acts for the relief of insolvent Debtors. it is Ordered, that the first monday in March next be assigned for said Cooper to be brought into Court to enquire into his insolvency, & that a copy of this Rule be served on the Plaintiff, or his Attorney, previous to the first Monday in March next, of which all the Creditors of said Cooper will take notice.

                                          Wm Rabun
                                          Jno Crowder
                                          Bolling Hall

Teste. Jas Lewis, Clk

                Hancock Inferior Court February the 2nd 1807   [210]

Present, their Honors   Stephen Evans   }
                                              John Crowder & } Esquires
                                              Bolling Hall   }

Ordered, That Tavern Licence be granted to John Freeman and Davis Smith to retail Spirituous liquors at their places of residence in this County for one year, Also to Willie Abercrombie to retail Spirituous liquors for one year.

Ordered, that John J. Davidson be & he is hereby appointed Overseer of the Road leading from Fulsom's Creek to Shivers's Mill, & the following hands work thereon, Viz.

Widow Huckaby, Sam[l] Barfield, Benjamin Cook, William Cook, Ezekiel Smith, John Andrews, Gray Andrews, Greene Andrews, Andrew Stewart, John Armstrong, Maximillon Armstrong, & Reuben Jones.

Ordered, That Tavern licence be granted William Garey to retail Spirituous liquors at his place of residence in this County for one year.

February the 2nd 1807 [211]

Ordered, That George Morris, a boy of Colour, be & he is hereby bound to Richard Respess, J[r] for three years.

Ordered, That the Sum of thirty dollars be appropriated and paid to [blot] Henry Moss for ~~Keeping~~ to be applied the support of William Burges, J[r] eight months.

                                        Stephen Evans
                                        Jn° Crowder
                                        Bolling Hall

Court Adj[d] until Court in Course.

Test. James Lewis, Clk

February the 16th 1807

Present, their Honors   William Rabun }
                                      John Crowder &} Esq[rs]
                                        Bolling Hall   }

Ordered, That Tavern licence be granted Starling Lewis and Edward D. Alfriend, William Hutchinson, James Andrews, Eli Harris & C°, James Waller, Jonathan Davis,

February the 16th 1807 [212]

William & Thomas Hudson, Samuel M. Devereux & C°, George Stewart, John J. Davidson to retail Spirituous liquors at their places of residence for one year.

Court Adjourned until 1st Monday in March.

Feby 17th 1807 James Lewis, Clk

Monday March the 2nd 1807

The Court met agreeably to adjournment.

Present, their Honors   William Rabun   }
                               John Crowder &   } Esquires
                               Richard A. Blount }

Ordered, That a road be laid out the nearest & best way from Mr Carr's lane to strike the old road a small distance from Mr Smith's Spring, agreeable to report of commissioners.

Monday March the 2nd 1807 [213]

Ordered, that the Sum of Six Dollars and fifty Cents be appropriated and paid to Docr William Terrell, in full for administering medicine to the poor.

Ordered, That James Bonner be and he is hereby appointed Overseer of the road leading from Sparta to said Bonner's, & the following hands work thereon, Viz.

Richard Bonner, Hubbard Bonner, Smith Cotton, Richard Garey, Hartwell Garey, Solomon Saunders, Richard Sasnett, Jn° Wilkerson, William Stembridge, John Turner, Robert Raines, Greenberry Pinkston, and John Kennon, Thomas M. Bonner.

Whereas, an attachment in favor of William Simmons vs Richard long was levied on a mare and the same being of a perishable nature.

It is Ordered, that the Sheriff sell the same after giving ten days notice at the Store of Williamson Reese in this County, and the monies arising from said sale to be paid into the Clerk's Office Subject to the further Order of said Court.

Ordered, That Matthew Durham, John Harvey, J^r, James Harris, Peter Hutchinson, and Ellenson Morgan be and they are hereby appointed Commissioners to view and lay out a road the nearest and best way from Samuel Breedlove's to Yarbrough's ferry on the Oconee, agreeable to a former Order of

Monday the 2nd day of March 1807 [214]

the 8th of January, be and the same is hereby revoked.

Ordered, That George Butts be and he is hereby appointed Overseer of the Road leading from Henry Graybill's to logdam Creek, & the following hands work thereon (Viz.)

Thomas Stembrige, John Mattox, Alexander Bass, Se^r, Green Mitchell, Lott Harthorn, Hubbard Brown, Benjamin Simmons, Senr, Andrew Jeter, Willis Mangham, William Donaghey, Henry Graybill, William Breedlove, Isaiah Parker, Tully Choice, John Rivers, Elizabeth Foster. iss^d.

Ordered, that Euclid Langford be appointed Overseer of the Road leading from the Academy old house to Baxter's Bridge, & the following hands work thereon.

Jo^s Chambers, William Thomas, Fred^k G. Thomas, Stephen Bishop, Abel Pugh, Thomas Turner, William Horton, Widow Swinney, Gabriel Moss, & Jecamiah Moore.

Monday March the 2nd 1807 [215]

The Court having heard the Petition of Joseph Cooper, Senr praying to be discharged as an insolvent Debtor, and the said Joseph Cooper having taken the ~~oath~~ necessary oath, it is

Ordered, that the said Joseph Cooper, Senr be discharged in Terms of the Act entitled an Act for the relief of insolvent Debtors.

Ordered, That Briton Rogers, David Lewis, & David Rosser, Senr be and they are hereby appointed Commissioners to View and lay out a Road the nearest & best was from David Lewis's machine, through George Smith's lane, to interesct Cooper's Road on the Stoney ridge, and report to the next Court.

Ordered, That a road be laid out the nearest & best way from Sparta to the forks of the Road where Benjamin Averitt formerly lived, agreeable to report of Commissioners.

Wm Rabun
R. Blount
Jno Crowder

Monday April the 6th 1807 [216]

Present, their Honors   William Rabun   }
                            Stephen Evans   } Esquires
                            Richard A. Blount }
                            & Bolling Hall }

Ordered, That Tavern licence be granted to McKinn Howell and Charles Medlock to retail Spirituous liquors at their places of Residence in Hancock County for one year.

Ordered, That the following hands be Subject to work on the road leading from the fork below Bunker's Hill to little Ogeechee (Viz.)

Francis Lewis, Senr, Richard Blount, James Wood, John Tillman, Richard Taylor, Jacob Holland, David Huckaby, Thomas Teagan, James Page, Washington Dickson, David Hitchcock, Burgess Williams, Silas Hodge, Benjamin Dickson, ~~John~~ Thomas Tyler, Joseph Wood, Levi Hendrikin, and John Dickson, Overseer of the same. iss^d.

Ordered, That the following hands be subject to work on the road leading from Mitchell's Store to Bivins' (Viz.)

Ben^j Brantley, Benjamin Hall, John Callaway, Abraham Borland, John Henderson, John Loftin, Benjamin Parker, John King, Elijah King, Elisha King, Wm Freeny, John Justice, Washington McLinsey, Timothy Sears, & John Mitchell, Overseer of the same.

Monday the 6th of April 1807 [217]

Oredered, That the following hands be subject to work on the road leading from John Harvey's to Powelton (Viz.)

Wm H. Mathews, John Colbert, Jesse Connell, Hardy R. Jernigan, Joseph Henry, J^r, Wm Connell, John Henry, J^r, John Henry, Senr, B. Henry, Henderson Henry, Wm Henry, N. Darling, Wm Darling, John Jones, John Lord, Nancy Stewart, Wm Brown, William Moon, & Hardy Jernigan, Overseer of the Same. iss^d.

Ordered, That the Sum of ten dollars be appropriated and paid to Samuel Hall, Senr, Coroner, for holding a inquest over a negro ~~dec^d~~ Woman Dec^d, the owner not living in the County. paid.

Ordered, That the sum of fifteen dollars be appropriated and paid to Joseph Bryan, fifteen dollars to Archibald Campbell, Deceased, & twelve dollars to Hines Holt, in full for their services as Commissioners for examining into the County funds, agreeable to an Order of the Superior Court.

Ordered, that the Clerk of the Superior ~~Court~~ and Inferior Courts [blot] the County of Hancock, the next Court to be held on the first Monday in May next, and that a regular return of same nature and report be made to every Court thereafter. together with a [blot] list of all other appropriations now made and to whom.

	R. Blount	Bolling Hall
Wm Rabun	Stephen Evans	Jno Crowder

Court Adjourned until the first Monday in May next. [218]

Attest. Ja^s Lewis, Clk

Monday May the 4th 1807.

Present, their Honors

Wm Rabun
Stephen Evans
Rich Blount
Jno Crowder
Bolling Hall

Ordered, That a Road be laid out the Nearest and best way from Sparta to where Ben^j Everett formerly lived, and that Robert Raines be appointed Overseer of that part Between Sparta and the road leading from Shy's to Pinkston's Mills, and that the following hands work thereon, Viz.

said Raines's, Mary Pinston's, Henry Pinkston's, Henry Moss, Green Pinkson's, John Tanner's, John Pinkston, Wm Stembridge, and [blot]. John Brown, overseer, from the above road leading [faint] Saw Mill to Everett's, and the following hands work thereon, Viz.

James Majors, Wm Gilliland, Richard Larnett, Wm Grantham, Isaac Dennis, John Turner, Morris Born, Ann Dent, [blank] [smear] Robt [smear] W^m [faint]. [smear] Peterson, [faint] Wilkens, W^m [illegible]

Ordered, That Benjamin Taliaferro, William Peace, Wingate Hart, [219] Richard G. Brown be and they are hereby appointed commissioners to lay out a road the nearest and best way from Holt's Mills on Town Creek to Averett's ferry over the Oconee River.

Ordered, That Robert McGinty be and he is hereby appointed a Justice of the Peace in Capt Graybill's District, in place of Hugh M. Comer, Esquire, removed.

Court adjourned until the first Monday in June next.

        Wm Rabun
        Stephen Evans
        R. Blount
        Jno Crowder
        Bolling Hall

     Chambers May the 20th 1807   [220]

Present, the Hororable   Richard A. Blount, Esqr }

Whereas, James Hamilton, late Deputy Sheriff, has resigned and whereas Hamlin Lewis, Sheriff of the County of Hancock, has thought fit to appoint William Lewis to fill the vacancy aforesaid occasioned by the resignation aforesaid. In conformity thereto, William Lewis came forward and was qualified, agreeable to Law.

        R. A. Blount, J. I. C.

Test. Ja^s Lewis, Clk

Monday the 1st of June 1807 [221]

Present, their Honors   Stephen Evans   }
                           Richard A. Blount } Esq^{rs}
                           John Crowder &   }
                           Bolling Hall   }

Ordered, That the sum of three Hundred and nine dollars and eighty five Cents be appropriated and paid to Benjamin Sandford, in full for the proportional part of Hancock County for repairing & building a Bridge across Ogeechee at Burches Mill. iss^d.

Ordered, That Tavern licence be granted to Leonard Pearson to retail Spirituous liquors at his place of residence in Hancock County one year.

Ordered, That John Jeter, Samuel Harris, James Hunt, Reuben Herndon, and Judkins Hunt, J^r be and they are hereby appointed Commissioners to review and lay out a road leading from the plantation of James McGrimes, dec^d to Turner Hunt's Mill on Shoulderbone Creek, taking special care not to injure the plantation of any person whose lands it may run through more than the utility of the road requires, & that they or a majority of them report to the next Inferior Court, together with a list of the hands liable to work thereon. issued.

Monday June 1st 1807 [222]

Ordered, That Risdon Moore, J^r be and he is hereby appointed a Justice of the Peace in Capt Waller's District, in place of William Bullock, Dec^d.

Also, Henry Bonner of Capt Youngblood's Dis^t, formerly Capt Holt's Dis^t, in place of Thomas Slatter, Esquire, resigned.

J^{no} Crowder
R. Blount
Wm Rabun
Bolling Hall

Court Adjourned until Court in Course.

Attest. Ja^s Lewis, Clk

Monday the 6th of July 1807

Present, their Honors   William Rabun   }
                              Stephen Evans   }
                              Richard A. Blount } Esquires
                              John Crowder &   }
                              Bolling Hall   }

Monday the 6th of July 1807   [223]

Ordered, That Tavern licence be granted to Samuel Hall, Senr, Benjamin Harper, John Burch, Philip Turner, & Issac Hill to retail Spirituous liquors for one year at their respective places of residence in Hancock County.

Ordered, That Risdon Ryan, an orphen child, be bound to James Thomas until he becomes of lawful Age.

Also, Hampton Ryan to Elijah Moore, J^r, also Elizabeth Ryan to Levin Lockwell, until they become of lawful Age, the girls eighteen.

William Blank[blot] having made satisfactory proof to this Court that a certain Estray hog tolled by William Trippe before Hugh M. Comer, Esquire was his right and property.

It is ordered, that the Sum of seven dollars eighty seven and one half Cents be appropriated & paid to said William Blank[blot], being the amount of sale, after deducting lawful fees.

Ordered, that a road be laid out the nearest and best way from James W. Graves ~~agreeable to~~ to Turner Hunt's Mill agreeable to report of commissioners and in manner in which they have marked it out, and that the following hands work thereon (Viz.)

Turner Hunt's, Judkins Hunt's, James Hunt's, Samuel White's, John White's, Reuben Herndon, & Francis Ross, & that James Hunt be Overseer of the same.

Monday the 6th of July 1807   [224]

Ordered, That Tavern licence be granted to Willis Shivers to retail Spirituous liquors at his place of residence in Hancock County for one year.

Ordered, That the road leading from Sparta to Cooper's ferry on the Oconee River by Benjamin Harper's be Continued as it now stands, and that all orders or parts of orders to the contrary be and and the same is hereby revoked.

Ordered, That William Alford, J^r be appointed Overseer of the Road from the Sign Post opposite William H. Mathews to the road leading by James Halliday's to Sparta and that the following hands (to wit.)

Robert Martin's, William Alford, Senr, Wm Alford, J^r, Owen Alford, Nicholas Lamb, & Saleta Askey's work on the same. iss^d.

Stephen Evans
R. Blount
Jno Crowder

Attest. Court Adjourned untill Court in Course.

Attest. Ja^s Lewis, Clk

Chambers Tuesday the 4th of August 1807 [225]

Present, their Honors   Richard A. Blount }
                          John Crowder &   } Esquires
                          Bolling Hall   }

McCleod & Ray }
      vs   } Ca Sa
Neill Ferguson }

On the petition of Neill Ferguson Stating that he is confined in the common Jail of this County at the instance of McCleod & Ray on a capias adsatisfasiendum and prays the benefit of the Acts for the relief of Insolvent Debtors.

It is Ordered, that the fourth monday in this month be Assigned for the hearing much of the above Petition.

Ordered, That Tavern licence be granted to George Gray, Birdsong & C°, John Brown, John Neives, Ja^s & William Waller, Dennis Doyle.

          Richd Blount
          Jn° Crowder
          Bolling Hall

Teste. Ja^s Lewis, Clk

      Wednesday 19th August 1807   [226]

Present, their Honors   Richard A. Blount }
            John Crowder & } Esquires
            Bolling Hall   }

Ordered, That William Hunt and Joseph Cooper, Hubbard Reynolds, John Cook, and John Danill be and they are hereby appointed Commissioners to Keep open the Oconee River from the rock landing to the Greene County line according to Law. Issued.

          Richard A. Blount
          Jn° Crowder
          Bolling Hall

Teste. Ja^s Lewis, Clk

      Monday 24th August 1807   [227]

Present, the Honors   Bolling Hall   }
           John Crowder & } Esq^{rs}
           Richard A. Blount }

McCleod & Rae }
   vs   } Ca Sa
Neil Ferguson   }

Ordered, That the defendant in execution be brought before the Court to hear & abide the decision of the same.

The Jailor having brought up the Said Neil Ferguson and it appearing to the Court that the Jail [blot] not been paid weekly [blot] an Act of the Legislature [blot]

~~Ordered that~~ [blot] Same be [blot]

And [blot]il Ferguson having been [blot] of his property

But [blot] and person and

Taken the Oath prescribed by Law for Insolvent Debtors.   [228]

Ordered, that said Neil Ferguson be discharged as an Insolvent Debtor, agreeable to an Act of the Legislature entitled an Act to carry into effect the Seventh Section of the fourth Article of the Constitution.

Jn° Crowder
Bolling Hall
R. A. Blount

Test. Fred Freeman, pro Clk

Monday the 7th September 1807

Present, their Honors

William Rabun	}
Stephen Evans	}
John Crowder	} Esquires
Richard A. Blount	}
Bolling Hall	}

Monday the 7th September 1807   [229]

Ordered, That Ezekiel Smith be and he is hereby appointed Overseer of the Road leading from Benjamin Sanford's to Mr Lamar's ferry on the Oconee River, and the following hands work thereon (Viz.)

Frederick Lipham, William Trippe, Hugh Comer, John Pitts, [blank] Clark, Senr, Wm Tankersly, John Hill, Dionitious Wright, Wm Preston, Samuel Hawkins, Aron Smith, John Watkins, William Emmerson, & Benjamin Sanford.

Ordered, That Daniel Waller be and he is hereby appointed overseer of the Road leading from Charles McDonald's to Lamar's ferry, so far as Benjamin Sanford's, and the following hands work thereon, Viz.

Henry Cagle, Jeremiah Mullins, John Bengay, Jesse Bundridge, Robert Pettigrew, John Harbirt, James Barrow, Lewis Brown, Solomon Smith, Micajah Wade, W^m McLemore, William Williamson, John Thornton, James Butts, John Daniel, George Evans, Wm Carr, & Nathl Waller.

Ordered, That John Tingle be added to the list of hands liable to work on the road leading from the Montpellier Road to Harper's Mill on Fort Creek.

Monday 7th September 1807 [230]

Ordered, That Tavern licence be granted to Joseph Carr to Keep a House of entertainment at his place of residence in this County for one year. paid.

Ordered, That Benjamin Anderson, John Evans, Daniel Lowe, and James Farley be & they are hereby appointed Commissioners to view and lay out a road from Edward Clanton's to George Strother's land on the Oconee River and report to the next Court.

It appearing to the Court that there is a mare in the possession of Lewis Graves, the property of Nathan Tait, dec^d.

It is ordered, that the Sheriff Sell the said Mare at the market house in this County after advertising the same ten days and the monies arising to be paid into the Clerk's Office subject to the Order of Court.

Ordered, That Samuel Harris be and he is hereby appointed Overseer of the road leading from Shadrack Roe's to Main Fort Creek at Tripp's old place, and the following hands work thereon.

Saml White, Turner Hunt, Ja^s Hunt, Judkins Hunt, William Hunt, Mason Howell, Francis Ross, Absalom Harris, Ed Oneal, Jno Bass, Wm Hargrove, Samuel Turner, Job White, Reuben Herndon.

Ordered, That the Collector of Taxes for Hancock County pay to [231] Josiah and Thomas Carter four Hundred dollars in part for building a Court House.

Ordered, That James Pinkston, Richard Sasnett, Samuel Ship be and they are hereby appointed Commissioners to view and lay out a road the nearest and best way leaving the Saundersville road between Bunker's Hill and Samuel Shye's meeting house the most direct way to Pinkston's Mill on buffaloe and thence report to next Court. iss^d.

Ordered, that Samuel Ransom be and he is hereby appointed Overseer of the road leading from the piney woods house to William Gay's at the cross roads, and that the following hands be subject to work thereon (Viz.)

John Driskill, Wm Mangham, Joseph Knowls, Maning Bolling, Samuel Lewis, Benjamin Barnes, Richard Strother, [blot] Strother, Amos Brantley, James McGee, [blot] Phillip Jackson, Isaac Elliot, & George Runnels.

Ordered, That Stephen Bishop, Marshall Smith, John Horn, William Brodnax, Samuel

Reid, Nathaniel Roberson, Nathaniel Kindrick, Asa Hearn, & Zabad Hearn [232] be and they are hereby added to the list of hands subject to work on the road from the academy Old House to Baxter's Mill.

Stephen Evans
R. Blount
Jno Crowder

Court Adjourned until Court in Course.

Ja^s Lewis, Clk

Hancock Inferior Court October 5th 1807

Ordered, That the sum of Seven hundred dollars be appropriated to the use of & paid to John Rymes for One hundred thousand Merchantable well burnt bricks for the use of building of the Court house. And that Bolling Hall, the tax Collector, pay that Amount So far as any public monies Are in their hands. paid.

Stephen Evans
Bolling Hall
R. A. Blount

Teste. Ja^s Lewis, Clk

Hancock Inf^r Court 20th Octr 1807   [233]

Ordered, That Tavern licence be granted to Richard Morgan to retail Spirituous liquors at his place of residence in Hancock County for one year.

Ordered, That Myles Greene be and he is hereby appointed guardian for the persons and property of Coleman Greene, Myal Greene, and Edmund Greene, orphans of Peter Greene, late of Brunswick County and State of Virginia, Deceased.

$$W^m \text{ Rabun}$$
$$Jn^o \text{ Crowder}$$
$$\text{Bolling Hall}$$

Teste. Ja^s Lewis, Clk

Hancock Inferior Court 2nd Novr 1807 [234]

Present, their Honors   William Rabun }
Stephen Evans } Esquires
John Crowder & }
Bolling Hall }

Ordered, That Miles Grimes and Samuel Barron have ~~have~~ liberty to retail Spirituous liquors at their places of residence in Hancock County for one Year.

Jesse Grigg, Esquire, Sheriff elect, Came forward and was qualified agreeable to Law, and took and Subscribed the following Oath, Viz.

I, Jesse Grigg, do solemnly Swear that I will faithfully execute all Writs, Warrants, precepts, and processes directed to me as Sheriff of Hancock County and true returns make and in all things well and truly and without malice or partiality perform the duties of Sheriff of said County during my Continuation in Office & take only my lawful fees. So help me God.

Jesse Grigg

Ordered, That a road be laid out the nearest and best was from Clanton's [235] road to Strother's ferry on the Oconee River & the following hands work thereon (Viz.)

Benjamin Anderson, Thomas Jones, Alexander Bryan, John Lowe, J^r, John Lowe, Senr, and that George Strother and that Daniel Lowe be Overseers of the Same. iss^d.

Ordered, That a ferry be established at George Strother's landing on the Oconee River. iss^d.

Ordered, That William Brodnax be and he is hereby exonerated from working on the road from Joseph B. Chambers to Baxter's Mills. iss^d.

Ordered, That Hamlin Lewis, Samuel Dent, Walter Hamilton, John Bailey, and John Sturdivant be appointed Commissioners to view and report the utility of the road lately Ordered to be laid out from Ja^s Greene's old place to Turner Hunt's Mill and return their report to the next Inferior Court. iss^d.

Ordered, That Peter and Gabriel Runnels, Orphans of William Runnels, [236] be bound unto Samuel Watts until they become of lawful age.

Wm Rabun
Stephen Evans
Bolling Hall
Jno Crowder

Court Adjourned until Court in Course.

Ja^s Lewis, Clk

Monday the 7th December 1807

Court met agreeable to adjournment.

Present, their Honors   William Rabun }
                         Stephen Evans } Esquires
                         John Crowder & }
                         Bolling Hall   }

Ordered, That Tavern licence be granted to Mitchell & Jones, Phillip [237] & Simms & [blot] Turner to retail Spirituous liquors at their places of residence in Sparta for one year.

Ordered, That Tavern licence be granted to Ambrose Jones to retail Spirituous liquors at his place of residence in Hancock County for one ywar.

Ordered, That Levin H. Ellis, an illegitimate Child, be bound to Levin Ellis until he becomes of lawful age.

Ordered, That Charles Henson, Charles Bradley, & Jethro Jackson be and they are hereby appointed Commissioners to view and lay out a road the nearest and best way from Bradley's field to the Oconee River just below the mouth of Shoulderbone.

Ordered, That William Garey, an orphan child of James Garey, dec^d be bound to

James H. Jones until he ~~becomes of lawful age~~ arrives to the age of [238] twenty ~~one~~ years, that is, the 5th of Novr 1810.

Bolling Hall Returned a receipt of James Thomas for the Sum of fifty dollars, being the Sum appropriated in favor of said Thomas, also a Receipt of Edward Hood in favor of William Ray for one hundred and Sixty eight dollars appropriated in favor of said Ray for building a Bridge over Buffaloe. Also, a Receipt of Willis Rhymes for John Rhymes for three hundred ~~dollars~~ and thirty one dollars appropriated in favor of John Rhymes for making bricks, the above Receipts amounting to five Hundred and forty eight dollars 82½ Cents, being the amount of money Rec^d by said Hall on a Governor's warrant in favor of the County and diected by the County to be paid as above, and

Ordered, That all persons wishing to have any road laid out or removed or an apportionment of hands to work thereon will attend on at first Monday in March and September [faint] in Sparta as the Court will

only attend to such business on those days. [239]

Ordered, That Hartwell Gary be and he is hereby appointed a Justice of the peace for the County of Hancock in the place of Henry Bonner, removed, in Capt Youngblood's district. iss^d.

Ordered, That Thomas Ford be and he is hereby appointed a Justice of the peace for the County of Hancock in the place of ~~Henry Bonner~~ Hartwell Gary removed, in Capt Turner's district. iss^d.

Ordered, That Charles Medlock be and he is hereby appointed a Justice of the peace for the County of Hancock in the place of Tisey Thomas, dec^d, in Capt Williams's district. iss^d.

Ordered, That one half of the General tax be levied and Collected by the Tax Collector for the year 1807 for County purposes, and also one fourteenth part of the Genl tax be levied & Collected for the use of the poor of the county.

Jn° Crowder
Bolling Hall
Stephen Evans

Monday the 4th of January 1808 [240]

Court met agreeable to Adjournment.

Present, their Honors   William W. Rabun }
                                   John Crowder   } Esq^{rs}
                                   Richard A. Blount }
                                   & Bolling Hall   }

Ordered, That John Lattimer be and he is hereby appointed overseer of the road leading from Samuel Barron's new store to fulsom's ford on Ogeechee River, and the following hands work thereon (Viz.)

Mathew Humphries, Thos Humphreys, Wm Humphrey, Willis Humphrey, Saml Howell's, Demsey Griffis, Francis Griffis, John Harwell, Loyd Kelly, Martin Prewitt, Russel Prewitt, David Smith, Isaac Birdsong, Robert Lattimer, Dempsey Hays, Isaac Blount, Thos Willis, Moab Blount, Jn° Lenoir, Lewis Lenoir, David Cook, James Willis, Jn° Parker, Jn° Pullin, Jere Lary, Leny Lary, Robert Hicks, Richd Curry, Jo^s Howell, David Clark, Henry Dunn, Chas Medlock,

M. Johnson, Wm Curry, Barwell Tanner, and Dempsey Howell. [241]

8.56¼
9
77.06¼

Ordered, That Tavern licence be granted William Sanford, Sampson Duggar, Thomas & James Crowder, Brown & Barksdale, Thomas Hudson, Ichabud Thompson, Carey Askew, & Darby Smith, John Freeman & [blank] Holt.

The Court and Justices of the peace attended and proceeded to the election of a Receiver of Tax Returns and Collector of Taxes for the present year. And on closing the Polls, it appeared that Samuel Dent, Esquire was duly elected receiver of Tax Returns and Anderson Abercrombie, Esquire, was duly elected Tax Collector.

Ordered, That the Sum of thirty dollars be Appropriated and paid to Hannah Asberry, an indigent and infirm person. Iss^d.

The Commissioners appointed to ~~lay out~~ review a road from James Greene's old place to Turner Hunt's Mill reported as follows. We whose names are

undersigned have reviewed the road that we were appointed to view and [242] think that it is necessary that there should be a road where we were informed it was laid off before by the Commissioners.

Ordered, That the Sum of twelve Dollars be appropriated and paid to John Weeks in full for services guarding Nathan Tait from Augusta Jail. paid.

Ordered, That the Sum of forty dollars be appropriated and paid to George Lynch for Keeping an indigent and infirm Child.

That the sum of sixty dollars be appropriated & paid to Casby Huckaby for keeping two childred till first January next, ~~or at the~~ provided either or both of the children die within the year, then in proportion to the time they live.

p^d $30. p^d $8 in full.

Ordered, That the Sum of four hundred Dollars be appropriated and paid to Josiah & Thomas Carter in

full for building the Court House of Hancock County. [243]

Ordered, That the Sum of forty five Dollars be appropriated and paid to Edith Williams for Keeping William Clark until the first day of January next, including all arrearages upto this time not heretofore appropriated.

Ordered, That Enos Mahone be appointed Constable in Capt Waller's District. And that Thomas Shivers be appointed Constable in Capt Candler's District, Benjamin Temple in Capt Turner's District, John R. Scott in Capt Winslett's District, John Mann in Capt Pinkston's ~~Dis^t~~ and Youngblood's District, Archelaus

Averett in Capt Willson's Ditto, Daniel Milan in Capt Harper's District, And that all other Constables heretofore appointed be and they are hereby Continued.

$$\text{W}^m \text{ Rabun}$$
$$\text{Bolling Hall}$$
$$\text{R. Blount}$$

Test. Ja^s Lewis, Clk

Wednesday the 6th of January 1808 [244]

Present, their Honors   William Rabun }
                                       Richard A. Blount } Esq^{rs}
                                       Bolling Hall   }

Georgia   }
Hancock County }   We, the undersigned, having been appointed by the Honorable this Inferior Court for said County, to examine and lay out a road the nearest and best way from Sparta to the rock-landing on the Oconee River, Do Report, That the road in future run and be established as follows (to wit.) leaving Sparta at the South end of Mitchell Street, then running a straight line through Solomon Rountree's field to a Spanish Oak, at the fence being a line free between the said Rountree & Charles Abercrombie, from thence a straight line to the brick yard, crossing the branch at the South West corner of said yard, from thence to the old road now in use, Keeping that road as now traveled till it strikes the rock landing on the Oconee River.

$$\text{James Thweatt}$$
$$\text{Cha}^s \text{ Abercrombie}$$

Ordered, That the Overseer of the road leading from Sparta to the rock [245] landing do open and Keep in repair the said road, agreeable to the report of James Thweatt and Charles Abercrombie, Commissioners of the Same.

Ordered, That the Administrators of the Estate of Martin Martin, dec^d do by the first day of February next pay into the hands of the Clerk of this Court the full amount of Money reported to be due the County of Hancock by said deceased made by the Commissioners appointed by the Superior Court of this County for the purpose of examining into the County funds.

$$W^m \text{ Rabun}$$
$$B. \text{ Hall}$$
$$R. \text{ Blount}$$

Teste. Ja^s Lewis, Clk

Wednesday the 6th of January 1808   [246]

Ordered, That Solomon Saunders be appointed Overseer of the road leading from Sparta to the rocklanding, as far as James Bonner's old place, and that the following hands work thereon (to wit.)

Isaac Wilson, Jane Hunter, Richard Bonner, Henry Bonner, Solomon Saunders, Richard Garey, Widow Garey, Smith Cotton, John Wilkinson, Thomas M. Bonner, [blank] Heath, John Abercrombie, Phillip Turner, Dennis L. Ryan, and Thomas Ford.

Ordered, That one half of the amount of the General Tax be levied and Collected for the present year for County purposes.

$$W^m \text{ Rabun}$$
$$R. \text{ Blount}$$
$$\text{Bolling Hall}$$

Hancock Inferior Court March 7th 1808   [247]

Court met agreeable to adjournment.

Present, their Honors   William Rabun   }
                                      John Crowder   } Esquires
                                        Richard A. Blount }
                                        & Bolling Hall   }

Ordered, That Tavern licence be granted to Lewis Alford, Willie Abercrombie, William & James Lewis, & Jamison Andrews to retail Spirituous liquors at their places of residence in Hancock County for one year.

Ordered, That the Sum of five dollars & fifty Cents be appropriated and paid to James Hall, in full for Iron Work done on the Jail of Hancock County. paid.

Ordered, That the following hands work on the road leading from Cooper's ferry to Greene's Old Meeting House (Viz.)

Joseph Cooper, Sarah Butts, Jn° Butts, Myles Greene, Judkins Hunt, Henry Greene, Coleman Greene, Myles Greene, Jesse Simmons, Jn° Moubry, Thos Hinson, Jesse Warren, Drury Thweatt, Andrew Edwards, & Burwell Greene Overseer of the Same.

Monday the 7th March 1808 [248]

Ordered, That the following hands work on the road leading from Greene's Old meeting House to Benjamin J. Harper's Mill (Viz)

Daniel Melson, Ja^s Simmons, George W. Smith, Widow Parham, Francis Moreland, John Ingram, Senr, John Ingram, J^r, Thomas Ingram, Thomas Edwards, Burwell Bass, James Childs, Joshua Wynne, & Benj^a J. Harper, Overseer of the same.

Ordered, That the following hands work on the road leading from the fork of the road below Bunker's Hill to little Ogeechee (Viz.)

Lucy Lewis, Richard Blount, Mrs Wood, James Tillman, John Tillman, Ja^s Page, David Hitchcock, Burgess Willis, Thomas Tyler, Aurther Ford, Wm Lewis, Jn° Capehart, Silas Herrington, Thomas Carliles, Ja^s Barfield, & Henry Pinkston, Overseer.

Ordered, That Robert G. Crittendon have liberty to turn the public road leading through his land to Turner Hunt's Mill, agreeable to report of Walter Hamilton, Henry Turner, & Saml Harris, Commissioners (Viz.) We report that we think it Convenient & elligable that the old road be Turned and laid out on or nearly on the line between Robert G. Crittendon & Samuel Harris.

Monday 7th March 1808 [249]

Ordered, That Walter Hamilton, Andrew Baxter, Henry Turner, & Francis Ross be and they are hereby appointed Commissioners to lay out a road leading to Turner Hunt's Mill on or nearly on the line between Robert Crittendon and Samuel Harris & report to next Court.

Ordered, That the Sum of one hundred & Seventy five Dollars be appropriated & paid to Solomon Rountree for hawling bricks for the Court House.

Ordered, That the following hands work on the Road leading from just below the mouth of Shoulderbone to intersect therewith Cooper's Road at Bradlies' field (Viz.)

Chas Linch, Ja^s Linch, George Linch, Ja^s Davis, Chas Benson, Jethro Jackson, Stephen Ellis, Joshua Ellis, Elisha Ellis, Mathew Childs, Jno Williams, & William Waller, Overseer of the same.

Ordered, That a public ferry be established on the [smear] of the Oconee River on the lands of the Heirs of Christopher Williams.

Monday the 7th March 1808   [250]

Ordered, That the Road leading from Powelton to Carter's ford on Ogeechee be established as a public Road, and that the following hands work thereon (to Wit.)

Isaac Battle, Overseer, Jno Veazey, Benj^a Battle, Augustin Potter, Hezekiah Blankenship, Jno Bryan, James Crowder, Josiah Askey.

Ordered, That the following hands work on the road leading from Mrs Hunter's plantation to Eilands' Mill on buffaloe (Viz.)

Wm Sanders, Thomas Monghon, John Moye, W^m McDowell, John L. Jones, Thomas Lancaster, Edward B. Brodnax, Henry Neccessary, Joel Reves, John Mann, Ephraim Whittington, William Brooking, Jesse Carter, Saml Johnston, John Moffet, George Earnest, Robert Hutchings, Frederick Archer, Trawick Denton, James Pinkston, Wm Clayhorn, Thos Lancaster, & ~~Robert Hutchings~~, Overseer.

Ordered, That John Caswell, an Orphan Child, be bound to Isaiah Parker until be becomes of lawful age. Also, that R[smear] Isham Parker, an Orphan, be bound to Richard Parker until he becomes of lawful age.

Monday the 7th March 1808   [251]

Ordered, That the following hands be subject to work on the Road leading from Baxter's Mill to the ferry on the Oconee, where the same was established by Jeremiah Thrower, belonging to the Heirs of Christopher Williams (Viz.)

Jn° Horn, Samuel Dent, Danl Lowe, Thos Jones, Burton Sanders, Danl Sanders, Ge° Strother, John Lowe, J^r, Jn° Lowe, Ben Anderson, Alex Bryan, E. Rogers, Fred^k Foster, Martha Sledge, Edward Clanton, Dolly Chappell, Benjamin Chappell, Henry Thompson, John N. Thompson, James Adams, Jesse Moore, Stephen Evans, John Evans, Laban Evans, & Benjamin Anderson, Overseer of the Same.

Briton Rogers, David Rosser, & David Lewis, Commissioners appointed to lay out and view a road running through George Smith's land, Report that they have laid off Said Road running from David Lewis's machine to George Smith's land.

Ordered, the Clerk of the Inferior Court enter into a Book to be kept [smear] by him to be proposed on the expence of the County and kept for that purpose a just and true Statement of the Credits & debits of the County and that the true ballance be summed up to the first day of all [faint].

Monday 7th March 1808   [252]

before the Grand Jury & from that day there be regular entries made of all appropriations made by the Court, and of all public money Rec^d for the use of the County.

Ordered, That the following hands work on the road from Baxter's Mill to the Greene County line (Viz.)

Philemon Foster, Trewett Foster, Nelson Harris, Cornelius Clark, Wm Clark, Robt Clark, Laird Harris, John Baxter, Mens Sledge, Nathl Tatum, Senr, Peter Tatum, Thomas Chappell, John Chappell, Jonathan Adams, Nathl Mathews, Thos Huff, J^r, Solomon Ferrell, Ransom Moore, John Brodnax.

Ordered, That Howell Williams, William Hill, and Alexander Bellamy be appointed Commissioners to lay out a road from Joseph Carr's to Mahone's ferry.

Ordered, That Benjamin Wilson be and he is hereby appointed a Justice of the Peace in Capt Willson's District, in place of Charles Medlock, removed out of the District. And that William Sanders be appointed a Justice of the Peace in

Monday 7th March 1808 [253]

Cap.t Pinkston's District, in place of Zephaniah Harvey, removed. And that Joseph Bryan be and he is hereby appointed a Justice of the Peace in Cap.t Waller's Dis.t, in place of Henry Dixon, resigned.

Court adjourned until nine O'Clock Tomorrow.

Ja.s Lewis, Clk

Tuesday the 8th March 1808

Present, their Honors   William Rabun   }
                        Richard A. Blount } Esq.rs
                        John Crowder &   }
                        Bolling Hall   }

Ordered, That Stephen Clements be & he is hereby appointed Overseer of the Road leading from Sparta to George Cowen's, & the following hands work thereon (Viz.)

John Clements, M.r Shackelford, Francis Burroughs, Ge.o Cowen's, Flournoy's hands, Jn.o Lucas, Richard & Harris Sandifor, Stephen Clements

Tuesday the 8th March 1808 [254]

Ordered, That the sum of five hundred dollars be and the same is hereby appropriated for the use of Josiah and Thomas Carter, in part for building the Court house, And that the Tax Collector be Authorized to pay the same.

Ordered, That the Tax Collector for Hancock County make a final settlement with the Clerk of the Inferior Court from the year 1804 up to this date, so far as they have monies in their hands.

Ordered, That James Butts, John Sturdivant, Henry Graybill, Sen.r, Benjamin Simmons, & George Rivers be & they are hereby Appointed Commissioners, being first duly Sworn, to view & lay out a Road the nearest and best way from

Barksdale's ferry on the Oconee River to Samuel Breedlove's & Report to September Court.

        B. Hall
        Wm Rabun
        Jn° Crowder
        R. Blount

Court Adjourned until 1st April.

Test. Ja^s Lewis, Clk

    Hancock Inferior Court May 2nd 1808   [255]

Present, their Honors   William Rabun }
            John Crowder & } Esquires
            Bolling Hall   }

Ordered, That Tavern licence be granted to William Hudson to retail Spirituous liquors at his place of residence for one year from the 17th Feby last.

Upon the Petition of Jared Burch, junior Setting forth on oath that he has lost two notes of hand given him by Nicholas Childers, one for the sum of one hundred and ten dollars, the other for the Sum of thirty nine dollars and Seventy five Cents, & praying that the same may be established, on motion of Counsel.

It is Ordered, that the said notes be established after advertising the same in one of the public Gazettes of this State once in every month for the Space of Six months, unless cause be shewn to the contrary within that time.

    Monday May the 2nd 1808   [256]

Ordered, That the Sum of forty dollars be appropriated and paid to Catharine Hendricken, in full for Keeping Thomas Vaughan, a bastard child, for the Year 1807. Paid.

Ordered, That the Sheriff of this County Summon a Jury of twelve freeholders to examine and assess that damage that Solomon Rountree has Sustained by the public road running through his enclosed ground and report their proceedings to the next Inferior Court.

Ordered, That Christopher Harrison, orphan of Pleasant Harrison, dec^d, be bound unto Robert Lucas untill he arrives at lawful age.

Ordered, That Leavin Vinson be & he is hereby appointed a Justice of the peace for Capt Williams' Dis^t, in place of William Cureton, resigned. Issued.

Ordered, that the Sum of five hundred dollars be appropriated and paid [257] to Josiah & Thomas Carter in part for building the Court House.

          Bolling Hall
          Jno Crowder
          Wm Rabun

Court Adjourned until first Monday in June.

Ja^s Lewis, Clk

      Chambers May the 2nd 1808

Present, their Honors   William Rabun }
             John Crowder & } Esquires
             Bolling Hall   }

Patrick Dankin }
Sur^g C^o &c }
  vs   } Ass^t
James Holland }

It appearing to the Court in this Case, that James Holland is Confined in the Common Jail of said County on a bail Writ and that the Plaintiff (who resides out of this State) his agent and Attorney have given no bond and Security for his maintenance and Jail fees.

It is Ordered, That the said James Holland be discharged.

          Wm Rabun
          B. Hall
          Jno Crowder

Test. Ja^s Lewis, Clk

Hancock Inferior Court July 4th 1808 [258]

Present, their Honors
William Rabun }
Stephen Evans }
Richard A. Blount } Esquires
John Crowder & }
Bolling Hall }

Ordered, That Tavern licence be granted to Irby Hudson & C° & James Robinson to retail Spirituous liquors at their places of residence in Hancock County for one year. Also, to Samuel Hall, Senr for one year. Paid.

Ordered, That the Sum of three dollars be appropriated & paid to Abner Barksdale, also two dollars each to Daniel Lewis & Benjamin Jones, in full for services rendered in guarding Henry Bryan from Warren to Hancock Jail.

Ordered, That the Sum of forty one dollars & twenty five Cents be appropriated & paid to Dennis L. Ryan for services rendered the County for Printing. Paid.

Monday the 4th of July 1808 [259]

Ordered, That the Tax Collector pay Thomas Foster the Sum of four hundred Dollars in part for building the Court House.

Agreeable to the report of the Jury appointed by the Inferior Court to Assess the damages done to Solomon Rountree by a road running through his field. It is Ordered, That the Sum of thirty seven dollars Sixty ~~Sixty~~ Six & two third Cents be appropriated and paid to said Solomon Rountree, in full for the damages aforesaid.

Ordered, That an order made by the Inferior Court binding Pleasant Harrison, an Orphan, to Robert Lucas be & the same is hereby revoked.

Ordered, That Hamlin Lewis, Esqr, late Sheriff of Hancock County, do pay unto Leonard Abercrombie, Tax Collector of this County for the year 1805, the sum of one hundred and Seventy five dollars [blot] fifty two Cents this day, or attachment will issue against him for a contempt of Court.

$$\text{W}^\text{m} \text{ Rabun}$$
$$\text{R. Blount}$$
$$\text{Stephen Evans}$$
$$\text{Jn}^\text{o} \text{ Crowder}$$
$$\text{B. Hall}$$

Monday third of September 1808   [260]

The Court met agreeable to Adjournment.

Present, their Honors   William Rabun }
     John Crowder & } Esq$^\text{rs}$
     Stephen Evans }

Ordered, That John Johnson be and he is hereby appointed Overseer of the road leading from John Harvey's to Powell's Creek & the following hands work thereon (Viz.)

Joseph Cooper, John Vinnington, Ja$^\text{s}$ Tiggs, Jethro Barnes, Francis Butler, James H. Garrett, Catharine Byrum, Widow Johnson.

Ordered, That James Askey be and he is hereby appointed Overseer of the Road leading from Thomas Cooper's to the Greensborough Road at Colquitt's, & the following persons work thereon (Viz.)

Widow Harvey, Burwell Helsman, John Harvey, & Henry Lucas.

Ordered, That the following persons have [blot] Tavern license to   [261] retail Spirituous liquors at their places of residence in Hancock County for one year (Viz.)

Jesse Traywick, from the 14$^\text{th}$ July 1808.

John Burch, for the 1$^\text{st}$ August   D$^\text{o}$.

William & Micajah Thomas 15$^\text{th}$ Aug D$^\text{o}$.

Isaac Youngblood   "   "   "

William & James Waller　　"　　"　　"

Ordered, That John Gandy be and he is hereby appointed overseer of the road leading from Joseph Carr's to Mahone's ferry, Agreeable to the report of Alexander Bellamy, Howell Williams, & William Hill, Commissioners, & the following hands work thereon, Viz.

Ben Wells, Ja^s Rountree, [blank] Herrington, Matthew Mathews, Fred Duffey, Stephen Wright, Wm Pleasants, Wm Harper, Wm Sal[blot], Howell Williams, Ez^l Manchin, Alex Bellamy, Isam Bonner, Ja^s Callinhead, Jo^s Hartley, Wm Flournoy, Jno Asher, Warren Jackson, George Gray, Wm Dismuke, Jo^s Carr, Jno Hudson, Thos Rivers, & William Hill.

Ordered, That the Sum of forty dollars thirty seven & half cents be appropriated & paid to Jeremiah Butts, Jailer of Warren County, for keeping Henry Bryan one hundred & five days.

Ordered, That Edmond Jackson be & he is hereby appointed Overseer of the Road from Fort Creek to log dam Creek at Jesse Warren's, in place of Willie Abercrombie, & the former hands work thereon.

Ordered, That Betsey Ryan, an orphan child, be bound to John Felps, until she arrives at lawful age.

Ordered, That David Lewis be and he is hereby appointed overseer of the road leading from his machine to George Smith's land until it intersects the road to Cooper's ferry, in place of Burwell Rogers, & the former hands work thereon.

David Parker, having made it appear to the Satisfaction of this Court that a certain parcel of Hogs Tolled by Solomon Rountree was his right & property. It is Ordered, That the Sum of forty Dollars be appropriated & paid to David Parker, it being the full Amount of Sales, after deducting lawful fees. Paid.

Ordered, That Richard Brown be & he is hereby appointed Overseer of the road Thomas Devereux's Mill to the Sparta road & crossing at the fork of Buffaloe Creek, & the following hands work thereon, Viz.

John Lucas's, James Thweatt's, Jnº Norsworthy, John H. Armstrong, George & James Stell, Widow Vinnon's, Wm Stanton, John R. Scott, Hen Thornton, Fred^k Archer, Sterling Bartlett, Thos Vickers, Stephen Pearson, Ed Brodnax.

Ordered, That Richard Morgan & Levin Vincent be and they are hereby appointed Commissioners on the part of Hancock to cooperate with such as may be appointed on the part of Warren to let the building a Bridge across Ogeechee at or near the Shoals, on such plan as they may think best, taking bond with approved Security of the undertaker, to Keep a good Bridge there for five years.

Ordered, That Henry Lucas be and he is hereby appointed Overseer of the road leading from to Greensborough from Hudson's to Henry Colquitt's field, formerly [blot]atered Kirk's, & that the following hands work thereon, Viz.

Jo^s Barksdale, Robert Lucas, Henry Colquitt, Ja^s Lucas, Risdon Moore, Sol Langston, Moses Langston, Thos Williams, & Jno Harvey.

Ordered, That the sum of one hundred & ninety two dollars & thirty Seven cents be appropriated & paid to the different Guards who attended the Jail of this County for the safe Keeping of Osborn Randle, agreeable to their accompts rendered as follows.

P^d Samuel Roach, Sergeant 23 days @ $1.50 pr day	$34.50
P^d John Freeman, 23 days @ $1.00 pr day	$23.00
P^d John Bennard, " " " "	23.00
P^d Elijah Hall " " " "	23.00
P^d Victor Liviller " " " "	23.00
P^d Francis Biggam " " " "	23.00
P^d Isaac Evans " " " "	<u>23.00</u>
	$172.00
Richard Sandifer, Serg^t 1 Day	$1.50
P^d P. L. Simms " "	1.00

Thoˢ Biggam	"	"	1.00
Pᵈ Thoˢ Foster	"	"	1.00
Joseph Hall	"	"	1.00
Charles A. Grant	"	"	1.00
Alexander Smith	"	"	1.00
Pᵈ John Bennard	"	"	1.00
William Talley	"	"	1.00
Edmond Evans	"	"	1.00
Pᵈ Henry Lundy	"	"	<u>1.00</u>
			11.00
Isaac Evans, Sergᵗ			$1.12½
John Hudson			.75
Pᵈ John Chambers			.75
Pᵈ Jaˢ Trippe			.75
Samˡ Butts			.75
Pᵈ Hugh Taylor			.75
			4.87½

Pᵈ Also the Sum of three dollars & fifty Cents to Jaˢ Hall.

———

Ordered, That William Hill, Thomas Rivers, and William Flournoy be and they are hereby appointed to examine into the utility and expediency of laying out Road [smear] the nearest and best way from the Corner part of Barron field (or the road leading from Samuel Devereux's to Mahone's ferry) to the Oconee River at Thomas Brodnax's, and report their Opinion on oath to this Court.

Ordered, That the Sum of Sixteen dollars Sixty two & half Cents be appropriated & paid to John D. Brown for services rendered the State in guarding Henry Bryan.

> Wm Rabun
> B. Hall
> R. A. Blount
> Jno Crowder
> Stephen Evans

Court Adjourned until Monday next.

Test. Ja^s Lewis, Clk

Hancock Inferior Court Sep^t 12th 1808

Court met agreeably to Adjournment.

Present, their Honors		William Rabun }
				Richard A. Blount } Esq^{rs}
				Bolling Hall }

Ordered, That a road be laid out the nearest and best way from Barksdale's ferry on the Oconee to Samuel Breedlove's on the road leading to Sparta, agreeable to report of commissioners, beginning at said ferry and keeping the road now in use by Wilie Benges, thence by William Heath's to William Hutchinson's, leaving his Cotton machine on the left, thence by George Rivers's, thence by Benj^a Simmons', thence by George Stephens', thence along the old road through John McCarther's plantation and formerly went to Thompson's Store, thence through Thompson's private orchard, into the road now in use to said Brodnax's.

Ordered, That Jeffrey Barksdale be and he is hereby appointed Overseer of the road leading from Barksdale's ferry to George Rivers's, & the following hands work thereon (Viz.) [smear] Sanders [smear] Matthew

---

Mathews, Sol Mathews, Redock Mathews, Abram Bain, Fred^k Duffy, Berry Patillo, Jere Philips, John Clowers, E. Morgan, Willie Burge, Jno Burge, Jno Dickins, Richd Parker, Mat Durham, Willis Mangham, Wm Huthenson, Wm Heath,

Wm Spivey, Senr, Wm Spivey, J^r, Thomas Edwards, Sol Mangham, Ja^s Mangham, Saml Wells, Lewis Parker, Isaiah Parker, Mathew Burge, Benjamin ~~Parker~~ Simmons, Elijah Frazer, Thomas Harden, Elijah Hearn, & George Rimes.

Ordered, That Ichabud Thompson be and he is hereby appointed Overseer of the road leading from George Rivers' to Saml Breedlove's, & the following hands work thereon (Viz.)

Th^o Clayton, Ja^s Easter's, Ja^s Clayton, Jo^s Thorp, Nat Eldridge, Jno Porter, Jesse Cannon, John Pricket, Wm Childers, Robt Vaughan, Ja^s Danielly, Jno Roe, Wm Roe, Joshua Frazer, Ja^s Cannon, Ed Pricket, Jo^s McFrisie, Ja^s McLamore, Senr, Ja^s McLamore, J^r, Edmond Butler, Jno McCarter, Neil McCarter, David Pricket, Ichabod [smear] Thompson, Martin Gray, Thompson Gray, Smith Davenport, Jo^s Douglass, Saml Breedlove, Abram Hutcherson, Robert Hutcherson, Jno Breedlove.

         Wm Rabun
         Bolling Hall
         R. Blount

Test. Ja^s Lewis, Clk

Hancock Inferior Court 7th Nov 1808

Present, their Honors   William Rabun }
            Richard A. Blount } Esquires
            Stephen Evans & }
            Bolling Hall   }

Ordered, That Tavern licences be granted to Allen Alford, John Brown, & Henry Mitchell, J^r to retail Spirituous liquors at their places of residence for one year.

Ordered, That Daniel Lowe, John Lowe, & Burton Sanders be & they are hereby appointed Commissioners to lay out a road [blot] from the Southern corner of Turner Hunt's plantation out of a late order road the best way to the foard on Shoulderbone Creek between White and Evans, thence between the said creek and Evans's to Burton and Daniel Saunders's, thence between Benjamin Anderson and John Lewis, thence the best way to George Strother's ferry, & report to the next Court. iss^d.

Ordered, That Joseph Carr, James Reese, & Malone Mullins be and they are hereby appointed Commissioners to view and make a report into this Court on oath, the utility of a road the nearest and best way from Joseph Carr's to Sheffield's ferry on Oconee River, having due regard to enclosed lands. iss^d.

Ordered, that the Sum of Six dollars twelve & half cents be appropriated & paid to John D. Brown, in full for services rendered as Deputy Sheriff.

Whereas, the late Grand Jury of this County, upon the information of the Clerk of the Inferior Court, directed the said Inferior Court to compel Leonard Abercrombie, late Tax Collector, to come forward & make a Settlement of all arrearages due to the County, and the said Leonard Abercrombie having come forward this day and exhibited his Vouchers and made a full settlement, it appeared that he had overpaid the County fifty seven dollars eighty seven & half Cents. And the same be appropriated & paid to him.

Ordered, That the sum of thirteen dollars eighty seven & an half Cents be appropriated and paid to John D. Brown for services rendered the County as Deputy Sheriff, in guarding Osborn Randle & carrying him

to Warren Jail, which is to be refunded by said Randle when Collected.

Ordered, That the sum of two dollars be appropriated and paid to Benjn Temples p^d, John Hall p^d, Nathan Cook [faint] [smear] for taking prisoner from Warren Jail to Hancock Court at August Term last.

Ordered, That the Sheriff Summon a Jury of twelve freeholders to assess the damage that John McArthur may sustain in Consequence of the public road leading through his enclosure and report whether the expence transcends the totals of the same.

          Wm Rabun
          B. Hall
          Stephen Evans
          R. Blount

Index

—
  Daniel, 109
  John, 9
  Joseph, 5
  Lucy, 104
  Robt., 117
  Wm., 117
Abercrombie, 31
  Abner, 31, 95
  Anderson, 106, 129
  Charles, 10, 11, 22, 30, 83, 130
  Chas., 130
  Edmund, 40
  John, 83, 106, 131
  Leonard, 12, 19, 21, 24, 30, 33, 47, 66, 88, 138, 145
  Willie, 10, 26, 30, 43, 45, 55, 83, 89, 104, 112, 131, 140
Acee
  S., 4
Adams
  David, 63, 70, 109
  Isaac, 103
  James, 134
  Jonathan, 28, 134
  Robert, 109
  Robt., 70
  William, 109
  Wm., 70
Adkinson, 7
Alen
  Philip, 5
Alexander
  Asa, 56, 64, 104
Alford
  Allen, 144
  James, 19
  Lewis, 131
  Owen, 68, 100, 120
  William, Jr., 120
  William, Sr., 120
  Wm., Jr., 68, 100, 120
  Wm., Sr., 68, 100
Alfriend
  Edward D., 112
Allain
  Wm., 94
Allen
  Freeman, 19
  George, 15, 70, 97
  James, 36
  Jesse, 8, 15, 36
  Job, 9
  Philip, 20
  Robert, 36
  Wm., 94
Almonds
  Starling, 7
Alston
  Robert, 102
Ammons
  Starling, 61
  Sterling, 77
Anders
  Jameson, 90
Anderson
  Abije, 15
  Ben, 134
  Benjamin, 63, 90, 109, 123, 125, 134, 144
  D., 71, 72
  Douglass, 76

Stewart, 76, 83
Andrews
  Gray, 16, 51, 112
  Greene, 51, 112
  James, 112
  Jamison, 131
  John, 48, 65, 112
  William, 15, 35
Archer
  Frederick, 133
  Fredk., 141
Armstrong
  ___, 9
  James, 51
  John, 6, 51, 112
  John H., 141
  Mark, 103
  Martin, 61, 77, 93
  Maxmillon, 112
Asberry
  Hannah, 84, 103, 107, 129
  Nathan, 107
Asher
  Jno., 140
Askew
  Carey, 128
Askey
  James, 51, 90, 139
  Josiah, 90, 133
  Saleta, 120
  Uriah, 68
Astin
  Wm., 105
Atkinson
  Abner, 39, 94
Austin
  Dempsy, 91
Averet
  John, 104
Averete
  Archelus, 104
  David, 104
  Jeremiah, 104
  Matthew, 104
Averett, 117
  Archelaus, 45, 130
  Benjamin, 45, 69, 99
  David, 45
  Jeremiah, 45, 78
  John, 45
  Matthew, 45
Averitt
  Benjamin, 115
Avrett
  Benjamin, 7
B___
  Alexander, 109
Bailey
  Alban, 9
  J., 20
  John, 17, 126
  Phillip, 61
Bain
  Abram, 143
Baird
  Edmond, 9
Baker
  Jas., 63
  Jas., Sr., 63
Baldwin
  Hiram, 91
  Wm., 94
Bandy
  Lewis, 21, 33, 103
Bankes
  Solomon, 8
Bankston
  Henry, 7
Barber
  William, 92

Barfield
  Jas., 132
  Saml., 112
  Solomon, 7
  Solomon, Jr., 32
  William, 51
Barksdale, 8, 12, 13, 15, 21, 26, 32, 36, 38, 53, 67, 68, 88, 98, 128, 136, 143
  Abner, 5, 51, 138
  Collier, 51
  Geoffrey, 12
  Jeffery, 17, 38, 54
  Jeffrey, 110, 143
  Jeffry, 8
  Jos., 5, 141
  Joseph, 20, 51
  Nathl., 64
  William C., 4, 5
Barnes, 45, 69, 108
  Abel, 65, 102
  Absalom, 5, 65, 104
  Benjamin, 124
  Ephraim, 4
  James, 4, 64, 65, 104
  Jesse, 65
  Jethro, 5, 139
  Joseph, 65
  Leml., 102
  Lemon, 65
  Lewis, 16, 34, 59
  Nathan, 4, 65, 102
  William, 4, 108
Barnhart
  Phillip, 63
Barns, 95
Barron, 19, 142
  James, 94, 95
  John, 6, 26
  Saml., 6, 16, 57, 94
  Samuel, 6, 15, 94, 97, 125, 128
Barrow
  James, 97, 123
Barrows
  James, 95
Bartlett
  Sterling, 141
Barton, 144
Bass, 67, 89
  Alexander, Sr., 114
  Alexr., Sr., 59
  Allen, 53, 58, 62, 65, 79
  Burwell, 132
  Jno., 123
  John, 101
  Starling, 96
Baswell
  James, 10
Battle
  Benja., 133
  Isaac, 79, 133
  Jesse, 20
  Jno., 104
  Lazarus, 21, 48, 55
  William, 35, 86, 108
Baxter, 23, 37, 40, 56, 63, 70, 71, 73, 75, 78, 90, 101, 109, 114, 124, 126, 133, 134
  Andr., 11
  Andrew, 4, 9, 11, 12, 14, 15, 17, 40, 56, 132
  Andw., 10, 14, 15, 16, 20
  John, 134
Bazer
  Edward, 5, 34
  Edwd., 8
  William, 8, 34, 86
Beach
  James, 5
Beale

Josiah, 5
Beall, 85
  Josiah, 4
  Samuel, 60
Bealle, 101
  Sol, 102
Beard, 29
  E., 61
  Ed, 77
  Edmond, 7, 15, 16, 61, 77, 85, 93
  Edmund, 69
  Francis, 49
  Fras., 29
  Wm., 108
Beavin
  William, 61
Beckam
  Zacha., 104
Bell
  Jesse, 79
  Nathaniel, 79
Bellamy
  Alex, 140
  Alexander, 89, 105, 134, 140
Bellerson
  Willis, 95
Bengay
  John, 123
Benges
  Willie, 143
Bennard
  John, 141, 142
Benson
  Chas., 133
  Isaac, 5
Betts
  Abraham, 33
  Joshua, 8
Biggam
  Francis, 75, 141
  Fras., 101
  Joseph, 75, 101
  Thos., 142
Biggham
  Jos., 83
Biggins
  William, 54
  Wm., 62
Bigham
  Francis, 100
  Joseph, 100
Birch
  Jared, Jr., 65
Bird, 15, 96
  Allen, 9, 27, 35
  Thompson, 10, 37, 39, 94
  William, 83
Birdon
  Benj. J. J., 63
Birdsong, 98, 107, 121
  Isaac, 128
Bishop, 64, 65, 104
  J., 73
  James, 66
  Jane, 54
  John, 63, 70, 71, 102
  Stephen, 114, 124
Bivin
  William, 29
Bivins, 16, 21, 61, 64, 93, 115
  John, 21, 90, 96
  Shadrack, 90
  William, 16, 29, 33, 88, 90
  Williams, 106
  Wm., 108
Bixby, 56
Black
  Richardson, 7
Blackshear
  Isaac, 93

Blank___
  William, 119
Blankenship
  Daniel, 36, 79
  Hezekiah, 133
Blount
  Isaac, 54, 128
  Moab, 128
  R., 103, 115, 116, 117, 118, 120, 124, 130, 131, 136, 139, 144, 145
  R. A., 117, 122, 124, 143
  Rich, 116
  Richard, 74, 76, 77, 79, 80, 83, 84, 87, 92, 93, 98, 99, 100, 106, 111, 115, 132
  Richard A., 27, 60, 61, 62, 71, 75, 76, 77, 79, 80, 81, 87, 96, 98, 99, 100, 103, 106, 109, 113, 115, 117, 118, 119, 120, 121, 122, 128, 130, 131, 135, 138, 143, 144
  Richd., 75, 121
  Richd. A., 77
Boatwright
  Thomas, 53
Bogue
  James, 10
Bolling
  Maning, 124
Bolt
  Benjamin, 31
Boman
  Ezekiel, 69
  Moses, 69
Bond, 13
  Henry, 6
  John, 6
Bonner, 30, 99, 105, 113
  Hamilton, 102
  Henry, 118, 127, 131
  Hicks, 90
  Hubbard, 10, 63, 113
  Isam, 140
  James, 9, 113, 131
  Jas., 63
  Jeremiah, 99
  Richard, 10, 30, 34, 63, 113, 131
  Robert Hix, 89, 108
  Thomas M., 113, 131
  Thos. M., 63
Booth, 13, 63
  John, Jr., 31
  John, Sr., 19
  Zachariah, 94, 95
Boothe, 95, 105
  Zachariah, 97, 99
Booty
  Nicholas, 40
Borden
  Benjamin J., 63
Borland, 27, 61
  Abraham, 9, 96, 97, 99, 115
  Andrew, 31, 97
Born
  Morris, 117
Boroughs
  Philip, 19
Boswell
  James, 31, 97
Bosworth
  Jacob, 29
Bott
  Benjamin, 6
Bowling
  Manning, 33
Boyce
  Else, 103
Boyle
  Peter, 9, 12, 46, 61

Bradley, 127
  Charles, 127
  James, 25
Bradlie, 133
Brantley
  Amos, 15, 70, 124
  Benj., 115
  Harris, 23, 40
  Malachi, 8
  Thomas, 8, 40
Brantly
  Thomas, 75
Braswell
  Bird, 54
Breedlove
  Jno., 144
  Nathan, 101
  Nathaniel, 86
  Saml., 144
  Samuel, 114, 136, 143
  William, 114
Brewer
  Isaac, 19
  Polly, 37
  Simon, 6
Bridges, 45, 46
  James, 42, 43, 44, 45, 92
  Jas., 44
  Joseph, 42, 43, 44, 45
  William, 81
Britton, 9
Broadnax
  Ed, 102
  John, 8, 78
Brodnax, 143
  Ed, 141
  Edward, 65
  Edward B., 133
  Edwd. B., 58
  John, 40, 134

  Thomas, 142
  William, 45, 124, 126
  Wm., 58
Brooking
  William, 133
Brothers
  Elisha, 53
Broughton
  Belitha, 52
  Joshua, 52
Brown, 41, 67, 80, 128
  Edards, 29
  Elisha, 52
  Epps, 34, 70
  Henry, 8, 40, 48, 92
  Hubbard, 26, 114
  John, 21, 23, 29, 32, 36, 40, 53, 67, 69, 88, 90, 94, 106, 116, 121, 144
  John D., 143, 145
  Lewis, 123
  Moses, 51
  Richard, 140
  Richard G., 117
  William, 38
  Wilson, 94, 101
  Wm., 29, 116
Browne
  Allen, 7
  Daniel, 15
  Epps, 8, 11
  Hubbard, 7
  James, 7
  John, 7, 8
  William, 7
Bruce
  Wm., 29
Bryan
  Alex, 134
  Alexander, 125

   Henry, 138, 140, 143
   Isaac, 10
   Jno., 133
   Joseph, 66, 116, 135
   Richd., 10
   Robert, 90
Bryant
   Jno., 104
Buchannan, 38
   Benj., 36
   Benja., 64
   Robert, 28, 38
Buckholts
   Jacob, 64
   William, 64
Buckles
   Jacob, 41
   W., 29
Buckner
   Benj., 9
   Charles, 36
   Chas., 15
   Joel, 8, 9, 38, 73
   John, 17, 28, 73
   John, Jr., 8, 38
   John, Sr., 8, 38
   Lester, 73
   Morris, 73
   Parham, 8, 9
   Richmond, 73
   Tilman, 29, 60
   Willie, 9, 38
Bullock, 21, 48
   William, 5, 37, 87, 118
   Wm., 102
Bundridge
   Jesse, 123
Burch, 36, 41, 101, 118
   Gerard, 79
   Gerard, Jr., 55
   Gerard, Sr., 79
   Jarard, 4
   Jared, Jr., 136
   John, 35, 69, 99, 119, 139
Burge
   Davis, 108
   Jno., 143
   Mathew, 144
   William, 108
   Willie, 8, 143
Burges
   William, Jr., 112
Burroughs
   Francis, 135
Butler, 52
   Charles, 86
   Edmd., Sr., 20
   Edmond, 90, 144
   Edmond, Jr., 20
   Edmund, 19, 21, 23, 26
   Edward, 7, 110
   Francis, 90, 139
   Henry, 52
   Jesse, 14
   John, 50, 52
   Thos., 15
Butridge
   Joseph, 7
Buttrage
   Joseph, 6
Butts, 114
   Fredk., 58
   James, 123, 135
   Jeremiah, 140
   Jno., 132
   John, 105
   Saml., 83, 142
   Sarah, 132
   Thomas C., 58
Byrom

Henry, 20, 52, 90
James, 20, 52, 90
Byrum
  Catharine, 139
Cagle
  Henry, 123
Cain
  H., 50
  Hardy, 50, 95
  James, 10, 58
  John, 9, 58
  Wm., Jr., 9
Caldwell
  Andrew, 83
  Ja___, 4
  John, 4
  Samuel, 51
  William, 4
Calhoun
  Ephraim, 53
  John, 10
Callaway
  Ebenr., 86
  John, 115
  Jonathan, 15
  Thomas, 94
  Thos., 108
Callinhead
  Jas., 140
Campbell
  Achibald, 116
  John, 52
  Thomas, 108
Candler, 88, 90, 91, 129
  Daniel, 88
  Danl., 29
  John, 29
Cannon
  Jas., 144
  Jesse, 144

Capehart
  Jno., 132
Car
  Joseph, 105
Carew
  Richard H., 61, 85
  Richd. H., 83
Carliles
  Thomas, 132
Carr, 82, 105, 113
  Jos., 140
  Joseph, 24, 88, 90, 123, 134, 140, 145
  Joseph, Sr., 105
  William, 88
  Wm., 123
Carroll
  Thomas, 26, 35
Carten
  Patrick, 75
Carter, 13, 133
  Abraham, 103
  David, 33, 103
  Farish, 29
  Isaac, 36
  J. Barrentine, 10
  James, 33, 58
  Jesse, 9, 58, 133
  John, 9
  Jos., 9
  Joseph, 85
  Josiah, 123, 129, 135, 137
  Thomas, 123, 129, 135, 137
  Thos., 9
  William, 6
  Wm., 9, 58
Cases
  William, 76
Casey, 85
Casstleburry

James, 61
Castleberry
  James, 9
  Richard, 16
Caswell
  John, 103, 133
  Richd. T., 53
  Thos., 53
Catching
  Benjamin, 29
  Philip, 29
  Phillip, 99
  Seymore, 41
Cates
  Thomas, 4
  Thos., 65
Cathell, 29, 64
  James, 41
  Levin, 64
Cato, 28
  Green, 64, 109
  Greene, 70
Catoe, 48
Cauley, 100
Cavanah
  George, 91
Cavannah
  Edward, 91
  Thomas, 91
Cavenah
  George, 29
  Thomas, 29
Chambers, 8, 9, 13, 19, 70
  David, 53
  John, 87, 142
  Jos., 114
  Joseph B., 12, 13, 37, 87, 126
  Robert, 53
  Robt., 8
Champion

Dubois, 94
  Henry, 103
  John, 50
  Nancy, 79
Chandler
  John, 40
  William, 48
  Wm., 97
Chapman, 89
  Benj., 16
  Benjamin, 69
  Deberry, 102
  Dubois, 94
  Hill, 94
  Isaiah, 64, 94
  William, 53
Chappel
  Benjamin, 109
  Dolly, 109
  John, 109
  Joseph, 63
Chappell, 73
  Benjamin, 134
  Dolly, 134
  John, 134
  Joseph, 73
  Thomas, 134
Chetam
  George, 57
Childers
  Nicholas, 136
  Wm., 144
Childs
  James, 59, 132
  Mathew, 133
Choice
  Tully, 50, 114
Clanton, 98, 109, 125
  Edward, 63, 90, 98, 123, 134
  Edwd., 109

Clark, 13, 21, 88
  ___, Sr., 122
  Cornelius, 134
  David, 57, 128
  Henry, 63
  Robert, 56, 71, 98
  Robt., 134
  Thos., 58
  William, 14, 20, 38, 56, 92, 93, 98, 107, 129
  Wm., 134
Clarke
  Thomas, 35
  William, 49
Claud
  Joshua, 83
Clay
  Nathan, 4
Clayhorn
  Wm., 133
Clayton
  Jas., 144
  Tho., 144
  Thomas, 82
  William, 87
Clement, 18
Clements, 11, 85
  David, 8, 22
  John, 45, 135
  Stephen, 135
Clower
  Thomas, 63
  William, 48
  Wm., 63
Clowers
  John, 143
  Jonathan, 81
Coffee, 108
  Peter, 19, 48
Colbert

  John, 4, 41, 67, 116
  Jonathan, 29, 64, 94
Collier
  Wyatt, 8, 16, 59, 88
Collins, 31
  Andrew, 75, 83
Colquit
  Henry, 51
Colquitt, 139
  Henry, 5, 101, 141
Comer, 31
  A., 10, 11, 14, 17, 20, 22, 24
  Anderson, 4, 7, 11, 12, 20, 23, 24, 25, 26, 27, 31, 32, 48
  Hugh, 122
  Hugh M., 68, 109, 117, 119
  Hugh Moss, 41
  James, 7, 31, 39
  Jamison, 6
  John, 10, 30, 33, 46, 47, 66, 88, 96
Conley
  Edmond, 78
Connel, 88
  Jesse, 4, 20
Connell, 91
  Danl., 51
  Jesse, 35, 41, 50, 116
  Wm., 116
Conner
  Jno., 108
  John, 64, 91
Connill, 62, 66
Connor
  John, 29
Conway
  Curtis, 82
Cook
  Belah, 29
  Benj., 16, 57

Benjamin, 35, 80, 112
David, 128
Hamlin, 109
Jno., 68
John, 19, 121
Nathan, 145
Philip, 29
William, 112
Cooksey
  Jesse, 76
Cooper, 16, 89, 111, 114, 120, 132, 133, 140
  John, 4
  Joseph, 12, 34, 41, 50, 58, 87, 89, 95, 100, 111, 114, 121, 132, 139
  Joseph, Jr., 19
  Joseph, Sr., 4, 68, 111, 114
  Tho., 20, 50, 51, 52
  Thomas, 34, 47, 49, 50, 56, 59, 62, 139
  Thos., 49, 55, 59, 60
Copeland, 9
Corley
  Edmund, 35, 41, 52
Cornelius
  Benjamin, 64
Cotton
  Smith, 63, 113, 131
Coulter
  John, 20, 21, 22, 23, 24, 25, 26, 27, 31, 32, 33, 37, 39, 43, 44, 46, 50
Courson
  James, 29
Cowen
  Geo., 135
  George, 8, 66, 135
Cowin
  George, 33, 36, 58

Cowles
  Saml., 101
Crawford, 40
Crittendon
  Robert, 132
  Robert G., 132
Crowder
  James, 48, 128, 133
  Jas., 20
  Jno., 69, 71, 74, 75, 76, 77, 79, 80, 83, 84, 87, 92, 95, 98, 99, 103, 106, 111, 112, 115, 116, 117, 118, 120, 121, 122, 124, 125, 126, 128, 136, 137, 139, 143
  John, 6, 8, 34, 66, 69, 70, 71, 75, 76, 77, 79, 81, 84, 87, 89, 92, 96, 98, 99, 100, 103, 106, 111, 112, 113, 118, 119, 120, 121, 122, 125, 126, 128, 131, 135, 136, 137, 138, 139
  Thomas, 48, 80, 88, 106, 128
Crowel
  Henry, 77
Culver
  George, 52
  John, 5
  Nathan, 103
  Salathiel, 52
Cummins
  James, 52
  Thomas, 52
Cureton
  Bolling, 53
  John, 53
  Rezin, 53
  William, 44, 53, 83, 137
Currie, 45
  Edward H., 45
  John C., 92, 94
Curry

Richd., 128
Wm., 128
Curtis
  Ephm., 104
  William, 45
Cuter
  Joshua, 16
Da___
  John, 9
Daney
  Francis, 66
Daniel
  Amos, 65
  John, 88, 123
  Levi, 13, 64, 104
  Nathan, 4, 64, 65, 104
Daniell
  Stephen, 37
Danielly, 14
  Arthur, 6, 14, 23, 27, 31, 105
  Jas., 144
Danill
  John, 121
Dankin
  Patrick, 137
Dansey
  Francis, 86
Darby
  Nicholas, 36, 79, 100
Darling
  N., 116
  Wm., 116
Darnell
  Henry, 75, 83, 94
Davenport
  Richard, 48
  Smith, 144
  William, 52
Davidson
  James, 13

John, 47
John J., 51, 72, 112, 113
Davis, 13, 55, 100
  Edward, 104
  Jas., 133
  Jonathan, 15, 62, 85, 97, 112
Davison
  Lemuel, 15
Dawson
  John, 27
Day
  Jonathan, 27
Debose
  James, 102
Deloach
  Joseph, 97
Dennis, 78, 83
  Daniel, 88
  Danl., 86
  Isaac, 110, 117
  Isaac, Jr., 69
  Jacob, 10, 31, 51, 58, 78
  John, 10, 15, 31
  Josiah, 40
  Matthew, 6
  Peter, 78
Dent, 73
  Ann, 117
  Peter, 4, 64
  Saml., 4, 68, 109
  Samuel, 5, 21, 73, 90, 91, 126, 128, 134
  William, 19
  William, Jr., 5
  William, Sr., 5, 62
  Wm., 51
Denton
  Edward, 9
  Trawick, 133
Derham

Matthew, 6
Derris, 29
Derrisa, 97, 105
Derry, 58
Devereux, 24, 30, 41, 78, 82
  Archd. M., 69
  Archibald M., 24, 30, 43
  Archibald McLellan, 21
  Jno. W., 11, 32, 66, 74, 75, 77, 89, 92, 95
  Jno. Wm., 24, 25, 31, 37, 43, 49, 60, 62, 63, 66
  John B., 10, 29
  John W., 23, 24, 27, 31, 33, 39, 43, 47, 76, 87, 92
  John William, 21
  John Wm., 20
  Saml., 10
  Saml. M., 102
  Samuel, 31, 142
  Samuel M., 48, 88, 102, 113
  Thomas, 140
  William, 6, 90
  Wm., 108
Dickerson
  John, 65
Dickins
  Jno., 143
Dickinson
  Henry, 4
  John, 4
  Wimburn, 52
Dickson
  Benja., 93
  Benjamin, 115
  David, 9, 35
  John, 93, 115
  Michael, 20
  Nicholas, 64
  Robt., 53

  Washington, 115
Dismuke
  Wm., 140
Dismuks
  William, 105
Dix, 19
Dixon, 13, 28, 36
  Henry, 12, 66, 102, 103, 135
  John, 45, 104
  Nicholas, 13, 67
  Thomas, 45
  Thos., 104
Dodridge
  Noah, 13, 23
Dodrige
  Noah, 63
Dollard
  Thomas, 69
Donaghey
  William, 114
Donnaghey
  John, 58
Doughty
  Ebenezer, 35
Douglass
  Joseph, 144
Doyle
  Dennis, 65, 75, 94, 98, 121
Drake
  Epaphroditus, 4
  Matthew, 86
Driskill
  John, 36, 124
  William, 36
Dryless, 91
Dubois, 94
  James, 94
Dubose
  James, 44
Duckworth

Jacob, 53
Dudley
  John, 64, 107
Duffey
  Fred, 140
Duffy
  Fredk., 143
Duggar
  Sampson, 19, 35, 41, 78, 88, 106, 128
Duglass, 9
Dunn
  Alexr., 17
  Henry, 128
  John, 69
Durham
  Joab, 9, 49, 61, 77, 92
  Mat, 143
  Matthew, 13, 114
  Slade, 8
Dysart
  John, 18, 19, 29
  Moses, 29
Earnest
  George, 133
  Jacob, 58
Easter
  Jas., 144
Echols
  Frederick, 70, 74
Edwards
  Andrew, 132
  Cate, 65
  James, 65
  Jeffrey, 65
  Loraney, 65
  Richard, 65
  Sally, 65
  Thomas, 132, 144
  William, 65

Eiland, 49, 58
  Isaiah, 19, 29, 90, 93
Eilands, 6, 9, 65, 83, 133
  Absalom, 65
  Asa, 65
  Enoch, 65
  Isaiah, 108
Eilans
  Absolom, 6
Eldridge
  Nat, 144
Elliot
  Isaac, 36, 124
Ellis
  Elisha, 6, 133
  Isaac, 52
  Jesse, 13, 52, 94
  Joshua, 133
  Levi, 52, 86
  Levin, 126
  Levin H., 126
  Solomon, 56, 60
  Stephen, 133
Emerson
  Britton, 5
Emmerson
  William, 122
Eppridge
  Jas., 53
Equals
  Fred, 8
  Frederick, 34
Ernest
  Jacob, 9
Erwin
  David, 83
Evans, 97, 144
  Abner, 70, 109
  Benj., 13
  Benjamin, 39

David, 70
Edmond, 83, 103, 142
George, 123
Isaac, 83, 141, 142
James, 8, 38, 73
John, 123, 134
Laban, 134
Stephen, 47, 49, 55, 56, 59, 60, 63, 66, 69, 71, 74, 75, 80, 81, 84, 87, 89, 90, 92, 96, 98, 99, 100, 103, 106, 109, 111, 112, 115, 116, 117, 118, 119, 120, 122, 124, 125, 126, 128, 134, 138, 139, 143, 144, 145
Stith, 70, 109
William, 8
Everett, 117
Benj., 116
Ewing
Samuel, 38
Thomas, 8, 38
Ewings
Saml., 8
Fagan
George, 93
John, 77
Thomas, 93
Fails
Arthur, 50
Farley
James, 63, 90, 109, 123
Felps
Davis, 90
John, 140
Fenn
George, 7
Ferguson
___il, 122
Neil, 121, 122
Neill, 94, 120

Ferrell
Archelaus, 29
Bird, 34, 82, 86, 87
Solomon, 134
Few
Ignatius, 95
Finch
Robt., 7
Fletcher
R. B., 20
Richard, 52
Richard B., 108
Flournoy, 135
John F., 98
Peter, 54, 89
William, 142
Wm., 140
Flowers
Edward, 33
Foard
Thos., 83, 87
Ford
Aurther, 132
Thomas, 8, 127, 131
Foreman
Jesse, 70
Foreson
William, 65
Forgerson
Henry, 109
Foster
___, 109
Elizabeth, 114
Fredk., 134
John, 63
John, Jr., 109
Levi, 90, 109
Philemon, 90, 109, 134
Phillimon, 63
Thomas, 46, 138

Thos., 142
Trewett, 134
Franklin
  Esom, 90, 108
  Esom D., 82
Frazer
  Elijah, 144
  Joshua, 144
Freeman
  Fred, 122
  John, 11, 18, 22, 25, 27, 33, 42, 44, 58, 60, 68, 69, 78, 85, 90, 91, 112, 128, 141
  Joseph, 105
  William, 29
  Wm., 105
Freeny
  Peter, 97
  Wm., 115
Fric___
  Joel, 10
Fulgham
  Stephen, 77
Fulsom, 7, 16, 35, 51, 55, 57, 73, 86, 97, 112, 128
Fulwell
  Richard, 7
Furguson
  Henry, 70
Gaither
  Brice, 8, 20, 22, 23, 24, 26, 27, 32, 33, 37, 39, 43, 44, 46, 47, 49
Galtney
  John, 53
Gandy
  John, 140
Gann
  Jenny, 48
  Nancy, 48

Garey, 131
  Hartwell, 58, 63, 98, 113
  James, 26, 30, 83
  Jmes, 127
  Richard, 13, 113, 131
  William, 112, 127
Garrett, 52
  Edmond, 90
  Edmund, 52
  Henry, 20
  James H., 139
  Mourning, 90
  William, 52
Gary, 70
  Hartwell, 10, 127
  James, 10
  Richd., 10
Gasper
  Mary, 24
Gay
  John, 8, 40, 41, 75
  Thomas, 8, 38
  Thos., 97
  William, 8, 15, 70, 124
  Wm., 97
George
  Elijah, 20
George III, 101
Gholson
  John, 19
Gibson
  John, 7
Gilbert, 51
  Martin, 5, 50, 51, 52
  Michael, 4
  Robert, 64
Giles
  Wm., 65
Gilliland
  William, 7, 69, 98, 99

Wm., 117
Gilmore
  Robert, 5, 39, 109
Gimble
  Jacob, 108
Gipson
  John, 16
  Thomas, 16
Glenn
  Robert B., 106
Godwizer
  John, 86
Gonder, 55
  Mark, 7, 16, 35, 47, 55, 57, 72, 73, 94, 97
Goodson
  Betsey, 107
  John, 78
Goodwin
  Young, 93
Goodwyn
  Lewis, 96
Goore
  Jacob, 64
Gordin
  Thomas, 8
Gordon
  Thomas, 18, 38
Goss
  Charles, 41
Gra___
  Richard, 95
Grace
  James, 7
  Thomas, 39
Graham
  Thomas, 29
Grammer
  John, 8, 40
Grant

  Charles A., 142
  Joseph, 35
Grantham
  Daniel, 61
  Danl., 77
  William, 7, 69
  Wm., 117
Graves, 15
  James W., 119
  John, 53, 54
  Lewis, 53, 123
  Miles, 89
  Samuel, 53
Gray
  George, 59, 91, 121, 140
  Martin, 144
  Thompson, 144
Graybill, 49, 66, 67, 68, 88, 117
  Hen., 10, 11, 15, 16
  Henry, 4, 5, 11, 14, 15, 20, 26, 50, 52, 60, 114
  Henry, Sr., 135
Grayham, 7
  Joshua, 7
Green, 108
  Allen, 61
Greene, 92, 132
  Alexander, 29, 41, 60
  Alexr., 64, 94
  Allen, 43, 70, 94
  Burwell, 132
  Coleman, 125, 132
  Edmund, 125
  Henry, 132
  Ish., 8
  James, 40, 70, 129
  Jas., 126
  Joseph, 9
  Miles, 70
  Myal, 125

Myles, 19, 59, 125, 132
Peter, 125
Robert, 35, 80
Greenlea
　Elijah, 29
Grier
　Reddick, 39
Griffin
　Dempsy, 7, 16
　Francis, 7, 16
　Henry, 77
　Thomas, 93
Griffis
　Demsey, 128
　Francis, 128
Grigg
　Jesse, 16, 75, 125
Griggs
　William, 34, 87
Grimes
　Miles, 125
Gunn
　Jacob, 97
　Richard, 50
Hadaway
　Thomas, 94
Hadway
　Thomas, 29
Hagans
　Thos., 105
Hale
　James, 7, 8
　Samuel, 5
Hall, 127
　B., 10, 11, 15, 17, 131, 136, 137, 139, 143, 145
　Benjamin, 115
　Bolling, 5, 11, 14, 40, 106, 109, 111, 112, 115, 116, 117, 118, 119, 120, 121, 122, 124, 125, 126, 127, 128, 130, 131, 135, 136, 137, 138, 143, 144
　Dixon, Sr., 66
　Elijah, 141
　Hugh, 66
　Isaac, 91, 110
　James, 23, 59, 83, 85, 132
　Jas., 142
　John, 48, 54, 86, 145
　Joseph, 142
　Kinchen, 79
　Saml., 57, 83
　Samuel, 39, 65, 69, 82, 87, 97
　Samuel, Sr., 116, 119, 138
　Wingate, 91
Halley
　Nathaniel, 49
　Samuel, 13
Halliday, 18, 101
　James, 51, 68, 100, 120
Hambrick
　Joseph, 5
　Thomas, 5
Hamell
　J., 12
Hamilton
　Duke, 10, 30, 34, 69, 70, 82, 108
　James, 10, 85, 92, 103, 106, 117
　John, 8, 24, 30, 34, 88
　John, Jr., 34
　Walter, 9, 21, 56, 70, 71, 126, 132
　William, 8, 16
Hamlin
　John, 7
　Richard, 23
Hammilton
　Walter, 109
Hammond
　Henry, 86
Harbirt

John, 11, 12, 38, 105, 123
Harden
  Thomas, 144
Hardwick
  William, 35, 86, 108
Hargrove
  Dudley, 40
  Dudly, 75
  Philip, 7
  Wm., 101, 123
Harper, 123, 130
  Benj., 15
  Benja. J., 132
  Benjamin, 119, 120
  Benjamin J., 40, 99, 132
  John, 15
  William, 8, 15, 40
  Wm., 140
Harrington
  Hardy, 53
Harris, 107
  Absalom, 37, 123
  Absolom, 101
  Eli, 39, 40, 81, 97, 112
  Elisha, 40, 102
  James, 114
  John, 91
  Laird, 134
  Moses, 9, 23
  Nathan, 93
  Nelson, 134
  Saml., 101, 132
  Samuel, 37, 118, 123, 132
  Simon, 91
Harrison, 26
  Christopher, 91, 137
  Fras., 31
  James, 91
  John, 16
  John, Jr., 7

  Joseph, 16
  Pleasant, 91, 137, 138
  Robert, 64
Hart
  Saml., 19
Harthorn
  Lott, 114
Hartley
  Jos., 140
  Joseph, 93
Harvey, 139
  James, 20, 26, 46, 50, 52, 110
  James, Jr, 36
  Jno., 10, 20, 141
  John, 51, 115, 139
  John, Jr., 114
  Michael, Sr., 35, 79
  Nehemiah, 10, 58
  Pinkey, 79
  Thos., 10
  William, 9, 13
  Wm., 10, 58
  Zephaniah, 9, 10, 57, 58, 135
Harvy
  William, 67
Harwell
  Jackson, 16
  John, 128
  Mason, 101
  Ransom, 17
  Samuel, 82
  Thomas, 16
  Vines, 60, 85, 88
Hawkins
  Samuel, 50, 110, 122
  Tho., 13
  Thomas, 29, 54
Hay
  Curtis, 67
Haynes

James, 15
Joshua, 40
Hays
  Dempsey, 128
  Dempsy, 16
  George, 16
Hearn
  Asa, 124
  Benjamin, 15
  Elijah, 144
  John, 109
  Thomas, 15
  William, 86
  Zabad, 124
Hearndon
  Reuben, 37
Hearne
  William, 33
Heath, 131
  Chappel, 63, 109
  Chappell, 70
  Colston, 63
  Kennon, 42
  Kennon B., 38
  Thomas, 90
  Thos., 109
  William, 143
  Wm., 143
Heister
  John, 19
Helsman
  Burwell, 139
Henderson
  John, 20, 50, 79, 91, 115
Hendricken
  Catharine, 136
Hendriken, 94
Hendrikin
  Levi, 115
Hennon

James, 93
John, 93
Spias, 93
Henriken, 23, 65
Henry, 41
  B., 116
  Benjamin, 41
  David, 37, 109
  Henderson, 116
  John, 41, 50
  John, J., 116
  John, Sr., 116
  Joseph, 4, 35, 41, 60
  Joseph, Jr., 116
  Wm., 116
Henryton
  Nathan, 6
Henson
  Charles, 127
  Thomas, 59
Hern
  John, 70
Herndon
  Joseph, 7
  Reuben, 101, 118, 119, 123
Herrikin, 74
Herring
  Alexander, 61
  Alexr., 36, 77
  Arthur, 36
  Sanders, 9
Herrington, 140
  Silas, 132
Hickinbottom
  Joseph, 4
  Thomas, 4
Hickman
  Abraham, 8
Hicks
  Robert, 128

Robt., 57
Higgenbotham
  Joseph, 102
Higginbotham
  Judy, 57
Hill
  Henry, 77
  Isaac, 27, 47, 49, 119
  Isaac, Jr., 27
  Isaac, Sr., 35, 72
  John, 5, 51, 122
  Robert, 64
  Robt., 29
  Thos., 64
  William, 134, 140, 142
  Wright, 70, 107
Hilsman
  Bennit, 90
Hinson
  Thos., 132
Hitchcock
  David, 115, 132
  Meshack, 65
Hodge
  Silas, 115
Hogg
  James, 29
Holland
  Jacob, 115
  James, 137
Holliman
  Harmon, 53
  Mark, 53
  William, 53
  Wm., 104
Hollyman
  Wm., 45
Holt, 41, 61, 66, 91, 94, 102, 108, 117, 118, 128
  Hines, 5, 116
  Robert, 4, 5, 64, 88
  Simon, Sr., 65, 102
  Singleton, 5, 48, 66
  Tapley, 5
  Thaddeus, 4, 5, 12, 56, 94
Hood
  Edward, 127
Horn
  Harris, 105, 108
  Jno., 134
  John, 124
  Levi, 51
  William, 53
  Wm., 7
Horton, 55
  Hugh, 23, 50
  William, 50, 114
  Wm., 102
Hosey
  Jonathan, 7
Howard
  John, 10
  Joseph, 38
  Wm., 9
Howell
  Dempsey, 128
  Hezekiah, 7, 16
  Jos., 128
  Mason, 123
  McKinn, 115
  Meshach, 57
  Mesheck, 16
  Saml., 128
  Samuel, 57
Hubert
  David, 29, 58, 61
Huchity, 107
Huckaby, 112
  Benjamin, 77
  Casby, 129

Charles, 49, 77
  Charles, Sr., 68
  David, 69, 93, 115
  Isham, 9, 61, 93
  John, 51
  Richd., 69
Huddleston
  James, 8, 38
Hudman
  John, 7
Hudson, 64, 65, 68, 88, 107, 141
  Allen, 59
  Erby, 9
  Irby, 56, 64, 138
  Jno., 140
  John, 142
  Thomas, 85, 104, 113, 128
  Thos., 9
  William, 7, 9, 12, 20, 60, 64, 88, 104, 113, 136
  Wm., 85
Hudsons, 104
Huff, 67, 91
  James, 8, 70
  Lundy, 8
  Thomas, 40
  Thos., Jr., 134
Hughbanks, 93
Hughes
  Dempsey, 27
Humphrey
  Benjamin, 86
  James, 7
  Matthew, 7
  Thos., 7
  Willis, 128
  Wm., 128
Humphreys
  Thos., 128

Humphries, 16, 21, 25, 40, 46, 48, 57
  ___, 95
  John, 6, 23, 26, 94, 96, 99
  Mathew, 128
  Matthew, 57
  Thomas, 16
  William, 57
Humphris
  John, 38
Hunt
  James, 37, 118, 119
  Jas., 123
  Judkins, 37, 119, 123, 132
  Judkins, Jr., 118
  Turner, 37, 101, 118, 119, 123, 126, 129, 132, 144
  William, 37, 121, 123
Hunter, 9, 10, 34, 37, 57, 58, 63, 133
  Janes, 131
Hurt
  Charles, 40
  Joel, Sr., 41
  William, 17
Hutcherson
  Abram, 144
  Robert, 144
Hutchings
  Robert, 133
Hutchinson
  Peter, 39, 114
  William, 31, 39, 112, 143
Huthenson
  Wm., 143
Ingram, 36
  John, 79
  John, Jr., 132
  John, Sr., 132
  Presley, 7, 89
  Thomas, 132

William, 72
Irwin, 29
  David, 9
Isle
  John, 53
Izzel
  Jesse, 57
Jackson, 20, 31
  David, 4
  Drury, 51, 61
  Edmond, 140
  Henry, 4
  Isaac, 4, 29
  Isaac, Sr., 4
  Jethro, 17, 59, 127, 133
  Job, 9, 58
  John, 17
  Mark, 7, 20
  Philip, 36
  Phillip, 124
  Stephen, 4
  Warren, 140
James
  William, 89, 107
  Wm., 94
Jarnett
  Richard, 69
Jasper
  Mary, 14
Jenkins
  Benj., 53
  Willie, 53
Jernigan
  Hardy, 41, 50, 116
  Hardy R., 116
  Henry, 20
  James, 41, 50, 79, 100
  Needham, 20, 41, 79
  Needham, Sr., 4
Jeter

  Andrew, 114
  Francis, 34, 86, 107
  John, 118
Jewel
  James, 74
Joels
  Richard, 65
John
  Danl., 77, 93
  Saml., 9
  Samuel, 42, 61, 93
  William, 7, 69
  Z., 15
Johnson, 36, 52, 53, 139
  ___, 9
  Charles, 9
  Chas., 58
  Danl., 34
  Israel, 54
  Jacob, 82
  James, 82
  John, 52, 96, 139
  Joseph, 8, 37
  M., 128
  Saml., 58
  Thomas, 59
  William, 20, 78
  Williamson, 58
Johnston
  Saml., 133
Jones, 56, 104, 126, 146
  Ambrose, 83, 88, 126
  Benjamin, 138
  Henry, 18, 94
  James, 8
  James H., 42, 47, 82, 127
  James Lane, 80
  Jas., 9
  Jas. W., 83
  John, 19, 50, 90, 116

John L., 58, 133
Joseph B., 56, 57, 60, 81, 91
Malachi, 57
Matthew, 21, 36
Reuben, 51, 112
Stephen, 86
Tho., 9, 109
Thomas, 65, 125
Thos., 78, 134
West, 15
Jordan
  Overoff, 61
  Richd., 105
  Solomon, 79
Justice, 108
  Dempsey, 29, 64, 102, 108
  Dempsy, 94
  John, 115
  William, 64
Kandler, 107, 108
Kelley
  Giles, 45, 61
  John, 15, 35
  Joseph, 93
  William, 90
Kelly
  Abner, 86
  Jiles, 77
  John, 64, 86
  Loyd, 128
  Robt., 64
  William, 91
Kemp
  Cecil, 16
Kenan
  Ann, 44, 82
Kenedy, 78
Kennedy, 53
  Caleb, 8
  Charles, 75

Seth, 47, 62
Kennon
  John, 113
Kilgore
  Charles, 35, 86
  John, 35
  John, Jr., 86
  John, Sr., 86
  William, 86
Kilpatrick
  Saml., 94
Kinchen, 49, 54
  Matthew, 33, 54
Kindrick
  Hezekiah, 9, 65
  Nathaniel, 124
  Samuel, 65
King
  Elijah, 105, 115
  Elisha, 83, 115
  Jno., 105
  Joel, 38
  John, 115
  Thomas, 15
Kinney
  Joshua, 5
Kirk, 141
  John, 9
  Stephen, 7
Kirkpatrick
  Saml., 64
  Samuel, 29
Knowles
  Joseph, 15, 33
Knowls
  Joseph, 124
Lamar, 26, 122
  John, 20, 25, 26, 31, 50, 94, 95
  Thomas, 23, 26
Lamb

Nicholas, 120
Lancaster
  Saml., 58
  Thomas, 58, 75, 91, 133
  Thos., 20, 133
  William, 20, 50
Lane, 102
  J., 102
Langbetter
  Joel, 10
Langford
  Euclid, 114
  Francis, 15
  James, 34
  Jervis, 54
Langston
  Moses, 141
  Sol, 141
Lankston
  John, 5
  Solomon, 5
Larey
  George, 97
Larnett
  Richard, 117
Lary
  Daniel, 15
  Darby, 15
  George, 16
  Jere, 128
  Jeremiah, 16
  Leny, 128
  Levi, 27
Latimer
  John, 7
Latimore, 13, 32, 48
  George, 57
  John, 15, 57
  Robert, 57
Lattimer, 65, 98

John, 65, 128
  Robert, 128
Laurence
  James, 19
Lawson
  David, 102
  Dudley, 102
  Francis, 31, 39
  Moulford, 102
  Thomas, 102
  William, Jr., 4
  William, Sr., 4
Lea
  Greene, 29, 35, 51
  Ransom, 29, 64, 94
  Temple, 51
Lee
  George, 11
  John, 107
  John, Sr., 79
  William, 35, 36, 60, 80
Leith
  John, 29
Lenoir
  Jno., 128
  Lewis, 128
  Robert, 39
Leonard
  Benjamin, 68, 100
  John, 100
Levar
  Philip, 24, 30, 34, 90
  Phillip, 91
Levare
  Phillip, 64
Lewis, 46, 49, 55, 67
  Archibald, 64
  Daniel, 90, 138
  Darling, 9
  David, 114, 134, 140

Francis, 9, 61, 77, 109
Francis, Jr., 17
Francis, Sr., 93, 115
H., 30
Hamlin, 9, 12, 18, 25, 42, 44, 55, 86, 91, 102, 117, 126, 138
James, 9, 42, 62, 66, 82, 83, 105, 112, 113, 131
Jas., 62, 69, 71, 75, 77, 81, 83, 84, 87, 89, 92, 95, 98, 99, 100, 101, 103, 106, 109, 111, 116, 118, 120, 121, 124, 125, 126, 130, 131, 135, 136, 137, 143, 144
John, 9, 17, 102, 144
John, Jr., 110
Lucy, 132
Samuel, 36, 124
Starling, 112
Sterling, 64
William, 9, 85, 117, 131
Wm., 82, 83, 101, 132
Linch
  Chas., 133
  George, 107, 133
  Jas., 133
Linebe, 104
Lingo, 108
  Elijah, 38, 90, 108
Lipham
  Frederick, 110, 122
Little
  Thomas, 64
Liviller
  Victor, 141
Lloyd
  John, 51
  Thomas, 7
  Thos., 10
Lockett
  Abner, 12, 16, 34

Jacob, 59
Lockhart
  Mary, 39, 94
Lockwell
  Levin, 119
Loftin
  John, 115
Logue
  James, 69
Long
  Alexander, 10
  David, 41
  Evan, 102
  Henry, 20, 52
  Jeremiah, 7
  Littleton, 54
  Richard, 113
Lord
  John, 116
  William, 35, 79
  Wm., 67
Love
  Andrew, 59
  William, 59
Lovet
  Thomas, 93
Lovett
  Richard, Jr., 16
  Thomas, 16, 61
Low
  Danl., 109
  John, 79, 90, 109
  John, Jr., 63
  John, Sr., 109
  Ralph, 4
  William, 71, 72
Lowe
  Daniel, 52, 63, 123, 125, 144
  Danl., 134
  Jno., 134

John, 63, 65, 144
John, Jr., 125, 134
John, Sr., 125
Obadiah, 82
Loyd
  Joseph, 64
Lucas, 13, 19, 21, 35, 36, 78, 85, 101
  Betsy, 35
  Henry, 51, 90, 139, 141
  James, 35, 41, 51
  Jas., 141
  Jno., 135
  John, 8, 10, 30, 34, 57, 84, 141
  Robert, 137, 141
  Tho., 20
Luckey
  John, 64
Lundy
  Henry, 142
Lyles
  Alex, 10
Lynch
  George, 129
Lyon
  James, 70
Maclemore
  John, 8, 25
Maddox
  Jesse, 4, 102
  Samuel, 5
Maddux, 38
  Joseph, 39
Mahone, 105, 134, 140, 142
  Enos, 129
  Peter, 95
Majers
  James, 61
Majors
  James, 7, 117
  Jas., 77

Manchin
  Ezl., 140
Mangam
  William, 15
Mangham
  Jas., 144
  Sol, 144
  William, 36
  Willis, 114, 143
  Wm., 124
Manley
  John, 52, 66
Manly
  John, 104
Mann
  John, 129, 133
Mapp, 102
  Housdon, 4
  Littleton, 51
Marbury, 40
Marchman
  E., 102
  Ryley, 103
  S., 102
Marcus
  John, 29
Marshall
  Moses, 12
Martin, 29
  Alex, 76, 83
  Archd., 83
  Mar, 14, 20, 22, 24, 25, 27, 31, 32, 33, 37, 39, 43, 44, 47, 49, 55, 59
  Martha, 73
  Martin, 8, 40, 130
  Patsey, 95
  Robert, 120
Mason, 13
  Jacob, 4

John, 52
Joseph, 52
Tho., 86
Thomas, 15, 35
Wm., 86
Massey, 85
Mathers
  William, 50
Mathews, 13
  Jeremiah, 95
  Matthew, 140, 143
  Nathaniel, 109
  Nathl., 134
  Redock, 143
  Sol, 143
  Thomas, 58, 78
  William, 24
  William H., 120
  Wm. H., 116
Matthers
  William H., 60, 68
Matthews
  John, 8, 66, 89
  Thomas, 65
  William H., 100
Mattox
  Alexander, 65
  Jesse, 65
  John, 114
  Saml., 64
May
  Lewis, 29, 64
McAllister
  David, 31
McArthur
  John, 145
McCarter
  Jno., 144
  Neil, 144
McCarther

John, 143
McCaughey
  James, 40
McClendon
  Joel, 11, 13, 14, 15, 16, 17, 18, 20,
    22, 27, 29, 30, 31, 32, 41
  Leven S., 29
  Marvel, 29
McCleod, 120, 121
McCook
  Alexander, 69
  Robert, 69
McCormac
  James, 6
McDonald
  Charles, 73, 102, 122
  Chas., 6, 105
  John, 49
McDowell
  William, 58
  Wm., 133
McFarling
  Thomas, 65
McFrisie
  Jos., 144
McGaughey
  Jos., 8
  Minn, 102
  Wm., 8
McGee
  James, 124
McGehee
  Davis, 5, 51
  James, 15
  Saml., 13
  Samuel, 18, 29
McGinty
  Robert, 13, 31, 37, 117
McGrimes
  James, 118

McK___, 94
McKay
  John, 37, 69
McKisie
  Jonathan, 7
McLamore
  Jas., Jr., 144
  Jas., Sr., 144
McLellan
  William, 48
McLemore
  John, 34, 70, 86
  Wm., 123
McLinsey
  Washington, 115
McNabb
  John, 109
McNeill
  James, 38, 42
McRay
  Daniel, 94
Medlock
  Charles, 115, 127, 134
  Chas., 128
Melson, 108
  Daniel, 59, 89, 108, 132
  Danl., 7
Mercer
  Wilson, 29
Merrel
  Peter, 5
Merrit
  Elizabeth, 36
Mershon
  Enias, 33
Michael
  John, 20, 50, 52
Middlebrooks, 53
  John, 24, 31, 46, 53, 78, 82
  Joseph, 109

  Micajah, 52, 94, 107
  Robert, 70
  Thomas, 70, 109
Middleton, 5
  Zachariah, 5, 26
Miflin
  Geo., 108
  George, 105
Milan
  Daniel, 130
Miles, 41, 47, 56, 64
  A., 94, 108
  Abraham, 29, 30, 89, 93
  Ann, 64
  James, 30, 47, 64
  Jeremiah, 29, 64, 94
  John, 11, 13, 18, 27, 29, 60
  Jos., 29
  Thomas, 29, 91
  William, 27, 29, 32, 49, 88
  Wm., 94
Miller
  Brice, 24
  Charles, 90, 107
  Edward, 54, 73, 93
  Elijah, 54
  George, 93
  Henry, 4, 51
  James, 57
  James, Jr., 7, 16
  John, 8, 15, 70
  Thomas, 53, 73
  Thos., 7
Mills
  William, 67, 70, 109
Minor, 62
Minton
  Joseph, 35, 86
Mitchel, 63

Mitchell, 35, 58, 65, 78, 86, 98, 104, 115, 126, 130
  Daniel, 79
  Green, 114
  Henry, 8, 30, 34, 70
  Henry, Jr., 144
  James, 30
  John, 42, 74, 79, 81, 84, 115
  Robert, 64
  Samuel, 79
Moffet
  Gabl., 58
  Gabriel, 15
  Henry, 54
  John, 58, 133
Moman
  Jacob, 64
  Plesent, 4
Monghon
  Thomas, 133
Monroe
  Isaac, 88
Montgomery
  David, 29, 41, 64
  James, 29, 64, 82
  Jas., 91, 94, 108
  John, 29, 61, 102
  Robert, 69
  Robt., 7
  Wm., 64
Moody
  Joel, 15, 36
Moon, 53
  James, 64
  Mark, 70
  Richd., 64
  William, 4, 116
Moore, 14, 27, 64
  Elijah, Jr., 119
  Ephraim, 6, 14, 16, 21
  Jacob, 105
  Jecamiah, 28, 114
  Jesse, 134
  Jonathan, 52
  Levin, 105
  M. Whitly, 105
  Mark, 46, 97
  Ransom, 134
  Richd., 4
  Risdon, 4, 10, 11, 12, 14, 51, 141
  Risdon, Jr., 5, 118
  Risdon, Sr., 5, 66
Moran
  Elisha, 29, 99
  John, 94
Moreland
  Benja., 94
  Francis, 132
  Fras., 59
  John, 4
  Robt., 59
  Turner, 109
  Wood, 64
Morgan
  E., 143
  Ellenson, 114
  Isaac, 70, 79
  Richard, 28, 36, 53, 124, 141
Morris
  Augustin, 15
  Benjamin, 65
  Buckner, 42
  George, 112
  Jas., 8
  Jeremiah, 105
  Nathan, 51
  Obadiah, 29, 95, 105
  Thomas, 96, 99
Moss
  Eppes, 27

Epps, 10, 76
Gabriel, 114
Henry, 11, 18, 27, 28, 83, 112, 116
James, 76, 83
Lewis, 10, 36, 48, 54
Mossey, 24
Motley
  Isaac, 70, 106
Moubry
  Jno., 132
Moy
  John, 58
Moye
  John, 133
Mullins, 24
  Clement, 24
  Jeremiah, 123
  Malone, 110, 145
Munroe, 85
  Isaac, 85
  Robert, 76
Murphey
  Jas., 7
  Jno., 108
  John, 29, 70, 91
  William, 35, 70
  Wm., 86
Musgrove
  William, 16, 18
Musselwhite, 24, 30
  Drury, 34, 58
  James, 30, 34, 53
  Jas., 82
  Sarah, 73
Musslewhite, 10
  Drury, 10
Neccessary
  Henry, 133
Neives

John, 121
Nelson, 101
  George, 64
  Ichabud, 78
  Jeremiah, 64
  Taylor, 5, 51, 101
Newsom
  Isaac, 38, 52, 71
  Joel, 71
  John, 54
  William, 54
Newton
  Isaac, 4
Nichols
  Jonathan, 10
Nolley
  Nathan, 91
Norsworthy
  George, 41
  Jno., 141
  John, 27, 58
Northarn
  William, 79
Northern
  William, 36
Norton
  Thomas, 25, 31
Oliver
  Charles, 86
Onail
  James, 8
  John, 8
Oneal
  Ed, 123
  Edm., 101
  Edmund, 37
Orear
  Daniel, 64
  John, Sr., 64
  Marium, 64

Wm., 64
Orrick
  James, 13, 49, 67
Osgood
  Daniel, 44
Ousley
  William, 4
Owens
  Beachum, 109
Page
  James, 9, 16, 61, 77, 93, 115
  Jas., 132
  Jesse, 9, 27, 36, 61, 77
  Lewis, 53
Palmer
  Elijah, 40
  William, 9
Paramor, 38
Paramour, 38
  Joseph, 28, 38
Pardue
  William, 53
Pare, 85
  Barnaby, 85
Parham, 16, 34, 58, 59, 132
  Nathaniel, 7
  Robt., 59
  Stith, 16, 89
Parker
  Aaron, 53
  Benja., 105
  Benjamin, 63, 99, 115, 144
  David, 94, 140
  Geo., 65
  George, 4
  Isaiah, 93, 114, 133, 144
  Isham, 133
  Jno., 105, 128
  Lewis, 144
  Mary, 12

R___, 133
Richard, 133
Richd., 143
Samuel, 13, 23, 29, 61, 64
Parmer
  Thos., 86
Parr
  Barnaby, 76, 88
Parrot
  Benjamin, 109
Parrott
  Benjamin, 70
Parsons
  Saml., 103
Pate
  Wm., 58
Patillo
  Berry, 143
Patrick
  Christian, 67
Patterson
  Jno., 77
  Joel, 9, 53
  John, 61
Peace
  John, 7, 38, 74, 88, 108
  Major, 42, 69
  Stewart, 94
  Wingate, 117
Peak
  Henry, 19
  John, 70
  John C., 8, 34
  John, Jr., 70
Pearson
  John, 62
  Leonard, 118
  Stephen, 82, 141
Peavey
  Abram, 10

Peek
  Henry, 19
Perkins
  John, 7
  Richard, 69
  Uriah, 69
Perkinson
  Drury, 54
Perminter
  Nathl., 78
Person
  Saml., 5
Peterson
  ___, 117
  John, 70, 97
Pettigrew
  Robert, 123
Philips
  Hillery, 9
  Jere, 143
  Solomon, 9
Phillip, 126
Phillips
  Hillery, 10
  Solomon, 27, 36, 61, 77, 93
Pickard
  Micajah, 27, 70
Pinkerton
  David, 10, 63
Pinkson
  Green, 116
Pinkston, 83, 116, 123, 129, 135
  David, 18
  Greenberry, 63, 99, 113
  Henry, 83, 116, 132
  James, 10, 58, 77, 123, 133
  John, 10, 63, 99, 116
Pinston
  Mary, 116
Piper
  William, 10
Pitts
  John, 122
Pleasants
  Wm., 140
Pogue
  Saml., 19
Pollard
  Robert, 8
Pommirson
  William, 79
Pope
  Allen, 38, 54
  Barnaby, 58
  Collin, 74
  Henry, 39
  Jesse, 39, 94
  Jesse McKinney, 59
  John, 20
  Quinney, 7
  Saml., 32, 94, 97
  Samuel, 15, 35, 73
Porter
  Jno., 144
  Joseph, 13, 29, 61
Potter
  Augustin, 133
Pound
  David, 54
  Joel, 15, 27
  John, 15, 36
Pounds
  David, 9
  Joel, 9
  Richard, 8
Powel, 19
  Cader, 78
  Jacob, 6
  Martin, 7
Powell, 139

179

Cader, 10, 31, 82
  Moses, 52
  Quinney, 59
  William, 15
Preston
  Wm., 122
Prewitt
  Martin, 128
  Russel, 128
Pricket
  David, 144
  Ed, 144
  John, 144
Pride
  William, 8
Prior
  John, 64
  Marlow, 64
Pritchett
  Philip, 16, 34
  Thomas, 45, 104
  William, 45
  Wm., 104
Pruit
  Maston, 57
Pryor
  John, 85
Pugh
  Abel, 114
Pullin
  Henry, 53
  Jno., 128
  John, 53
  Saml., 53
Purify
  Arrenton, 41
  John, 7
Rabun, 24
  Matthew, 35, 86
  William, 32, 33, 35, 36, 37, 39, 43, 44, 47, 49, 56, 59, 66, 69, 71, 75, 77, 79, 80, 81, 84, 86, 87, 92, 96, 99, 100, 103, 106, 111, 112, 113, 115, 119, 122, 125, 126, 130, 131, 135, 136, 137, 138, 139, 143, 144
  William W., 128
  Wm., 33, 37, 39, 43, 44, 46, 49, 51, 54, 55, 59, 60, 62, 63, 66, 69, 71, 74, 75, 76, 79, 80, 81, 83, 84, 87, 89, 98, 99, 103, 106, 111, 115, 116, 117, 118, 125, 126, 130, 131, 136, 137, 139, 143, 144, 145
Rachels
  Burwell, 45, 104
  Geo., 104
  George, 45
  William, 45
  Wm., 104
Rae, 121
  James, 59
Ragan
  John, 6, 46, 53
Raines, 116
  Cadwall, 29
  Robert, 63, 113, 116
Rains
  Robert, 10
Randall, 52
  John, 52
Randle, 145
  John, 88
  Osborn, 141, 145
Randolph
  James, 20
Ransom
  Robert, 52
  Samuel, 124

Rasbury
  Benjamin, 52
Rawles
  Abram, 80
  Philip, 16
Ray, 120, 127
  Frederick, 40
  William, 92, 127
Reddin, 50
  Nancy, 34, 50
Redding
  Nancy, 19, 79
Reddock
  James, 45
Reed, 32
  Alexander, 8
  Saml., 8
Rees
  Shadrack, 101
Reese, 85, 101
  Anderson, 8
  Drury, 103
  Howell A., 38
  Howell Anderson, 39
  Isham, 8, 40
  James, 40, 145
  Jas., 8
  Joel, 17
  Joseph, 38, 42
  Littleton, 17, 36, 66
  William, 4, 8, 9, 10, 30, 34
  Williamson, 113
  Wm., 102
Reid, 13, 21, 100
  Abner, 37
  Ajonadab, 19
  Alexander, 40
  James, 40
  John, 6, 40
  Samuel, 124

Respess
  Richard, 8, 40
  Richard, Jr., 112
Reves
  Joel, 133
Reynolds, 96
  Herbert, 96
  Hubbard, 121
  Hubert, 37, 88
Rhodes
  William, 29
Rhymes
  John, 127
  Willis, 127
Richardson, 102
  Francis, 5
  Gabl., 103
  George, 86
  Newman, 86, 101
  O., 102
  Obadiah, 4, 5, 36, 65, 66, 102
Rimes
  George, 144
Rivers
  George, 135, 143, 144
  John, 26, 49, 50, 67, 96, 114
  Robert, 66
  Thomas, 37, 110, 142
  Thos., 140
Roach
  Samuel, 141
Roan
  Milly, 20
Robbins
  Nicholas, 64
Roberson
  Nathaniel, 124
Robert
  Lindzey, 83
Roberts

Joseph, 79
Lindsay, 31, 34, 58
Robertson, 29
Frier, 36
Robinson
James, 138
Roe
Jno., 144
John, 6, 7
Shadrach, 40
Shadrack, 8, 71, 123
Wm., 144
Rogers, 94
Britain, 17
Briton, 114, 134
Burwell, 17, 140
Dread, 98
Dred, 82
E., 134
Elisha, 42, 44
Elizabeth, 104
Ephraim, 109
John, 19
Michael, 29, 64
Peleg, 90
Simon, 94
Rositer
Appleton, 10
Timothy, 10
Ross
Francis, 37, 101, 119, 123, 132
James, 7, 23, 40
Rosser
David, 134
David, Sr., 114
Isaac, 104
Rossiter
Timothy W., 34
Rountree, 130
Jas., 140

Solomon, 75, 130, 133, 136, 138, 140
Rowles
Abram, 80
Rudisell
John, 34, 50
Runnels
Gabriel, 126
George, 40, 124
Peter, 126
Richard, 20, 52
William, 34, 126
Russel, 31
Russell
Andrew, 82
Rutland
Randolph, 19, 20, 34, 50, 52, 62, 66
Ryan
Betsey, 140
Dennis L., 75, 83, 84, 85, 93, 105, 131, 138
Elizabeth, 119
Hampton, 119
Risdon, 119
Ryley
James, 90
Rymes
John, 124
Sal___
Wm., 140
Sallard
William, 34
Wm., 8
Sampson
George, 94
Sanders, 55
___, 143
Burton, 90, 134, 144
Daniel, 90

Danl., 134
Lewis, 89
Nathan, 104
William, 134
Wm., 133
Sandfd.
  Wm., 76
Sandford
  Benjamin, 118
  William, 85
Sandifer
  Richard, 141
Sandifor
  Harris, 135
  Richard, 135
Sanford
  Benjamin, 122
  Frederick, 42, 46, 76
  Fredk., 83
  Jesse, 26, 31
  William, 10, 42, 62, 104, 128
  Wm., 83
Sasnett
  Richard, 63, 113, 123
Saterwhite
  Thomas, 7
Saunders
  Absalom, 57
  Burton, 109, 144
  Daniel, 144
  James, 18, 40
  Jas., 8
  John, 8, 18
  Lewis, 59
  Mark, 7
  Nathan, 6, 7, 34
  Peter, 8
  Solomon, 113, 131
  William, 25, 57, 58
  Wm., 9

Savage
  Starling, 42, 86, 97
  Sterling, 94
Scarlett, 25, 30
  James, 21, 24, 25, 46
Scott, 13
  Frederick, 10
  Jas., 10
  John, 10
  John R., 129, 141
  Thos., 64, 68
  Woodlief, 10, 64
Seale
  Thomas, 84
  William, 35
Seales
  Danl., 86
  Spencer, 86
  Thomas, 86
  William, 70
  Wm., 86
Seals
  Archibald, 86
  Danl., 15
  Spencer, 15
  William, 15
Sears
  Timothy, 115
Self
  Elisha, 40
Shackelford, 135
  Frances, 40
Shackleford
  James, 109
  Jas., 8
Sharpe
  William, 17
  Wm., 59
Sheffield, 145
  William, 7, 90

Shells
  Byren, 109
Sherman
  John M., 42
Shi
  Saml., 23, 26, 35
  Samuel, 69
Ship
  David, 52
  Samuel, 123
Shipp
  Richard, 61, 86
Shivers, 80, 108, 112
  Barnaby, 8, 26, 38, 49, 68, 86, 94
  Jesse, 107
  Jonas, 35, 94
  Thomas, 129
  William, 94
  Willis, 35, 86, 94, 97, 119
Shoars
  Planner, 102
Shockley
  Thomas, 33
Shores
  Phlaner, 5
Shorter
  James, 22
  Russel, 111
Shoulders
  David, 45, 104
  Ed, 104
  Edward, 45
  John, 45, 104
Shuffield
  William, 16, 97
Shy, 116
  James, 9
  Jas., 77
Shye
  James, 61, 93

Samuel, 86, 123
Simon, 93
Simmon, 67
Simmons, 67
  B., 50
  Benja., 143
  Benjamin, 50, 135, 144
  Benjamin, Sr., 114
  George, 59
  James, 19, 58
  Jas., 132
  Jesse, 132
  John, 7, 35
  Robert, 59
  Tho., 59
  Thomas, 48, 88, 107
  William, 113
Simms, 126
  Joseph, 103
  P. L., 141
  Philip L., 103
  Robert, 20, 52, 91
Simons
  John, 95
Simpson
  George, 29, 64
  Nathan, 57
Singleton
  Hezekiah, 109
  James, 63
Sinson
  Zadoc, 8
Skelly
  William, 52
Slatter
  Thomas, 118
  Thomas J., 91
Slaughter, 48, 51
  Daniel, 64
  Danl. Candler, 29

Reuben, 51
Saml., 94
Samuel, 18, 29, 64, 102
Slave
  Ben, 45, 85
Sledge
  Chappel, 90, 109
  Chappell, 63
  Elizabeth, 63
  John, 63, 90
  Martha, 109, 134
  Mens, 134
  Minns, 82, 98
  Peyton, 70
  Shirley, 82
Sledges
  Elizabeth, 90
  John, 90
Slocomb, 88
  John C., 83
Slocum, 67
Smith, 95, 107, 113
  Abraham, 45, 104
  Alexander, 142
  Archd., 17
  Aron, 108, 122
  Daniel D., 79
  Darby, 128
  David, 128
  Davis, 77, 93, 112
  Ezekiel, 61, 112, 122
  Ezekiel, Sr., 51
  Francis, 36, 90, 91, 108
  Geo., 59
  George, 89, 114, 134, 140
  George W., 132
  Hardy, 6, 53
  Isham, 6
  Jesse, 79
  John, 6, 17, 26, 51, 73

  Joseph, 72
  Lewis, 63
  Marshall, 124
  Mary, 17
  Nathan, 52
  Nehemiah, 45, 104
  Richd., 10
  Solomon, 123
  Thomas, 14, 42, 54, 71, 72, 73, 76, 81
  William, 10, 76
  Willie, 8
  Wm., 71, 72
Sollar
  Simson, 10
Speckard
  Jacob, 29
Speight
  Levi, 35
  William, 35
Spencer
  John T., 8
Sperling
  John, 5
Spight
  John, 86
  Levi, 86
  William, 86
Spikes, 38
Spivey
  Wm., Jr., 144
  Wm., Sr., 144
Stanton
  John, 31, 34, 55
  William, 34, 74, 103
  Wm., 141
Starn
  Mary, 14
Staunton
  John, 8

Stein
  Mary, 23
Stell, 82
  George, 141
  James, 141
  John, 30
  Robert, 30, 34
  Robt., 10, 58
Stembridge
  William, 10, 113
  Wm., 63, 116
Stembrige
  Thomas, 114
Stephens, 58
  Elijah, 19
  George, 31, 143
  John, 110
  Thomas, 19, 31, 39
Stewart
  Andrew, 51, 61, 112
  Charles, 70
  Chas., 15
  George, 82, 113
  Nancy, 41, 116
Stinson
  Zadok, 40
Stith, 8, 15, 16, 18, 38, 51, 57, 61, 62
Stoneham
  James, 7
Stonham
  Bryan, 7
Strauther
  Aaron, 15
  George, 15
  Richard, 15
Strawder
  Geo., 109
Strickland
  Joseph, 6

Robert, 6
Thomas, 6
Stripling
  Robt., 104
Strother, 32, 36, 48, 124, 125
  Aaron, 36
  David, 36
  Geo., 134
  George, 36, 123, 125, 126, 144
  Richard, 36, 124
Sturdivant
  Charles, 68, 86
  John, 7, 59, 126, 135
  Patsy, 39
  Susannah, 93
Swinney, 25, 114
  Joachim Dudley, 25
T___
  Benjamin, 29
Tait
  Nathan, 22, 103, 123, 129
  Nathaniel, 102
Talbert, 105
  Jesse, 16, 21, 29, 41, 94, 102, 105
  Silas, 64
  Thomas, 64, 94
Taliaferro, 21, 32, 49, 100
  Benjamin, 117
Talley
  William, 142
Tamison
  Richard, 73
Tankersly
  Wm., 122
Tanner
  Barwell, 128
  John, 116
  Lewis, 16, 86
Tannin
  Lewis, 7

Tate
 Nathan, 18
 Robert, 28
 Robt., 53
Tatum
 John, 8
 Nathl., Sr., 134
 Peter, 134
 Seth, 64
Taylor, 47, 83
 Chas., 51
 Edmund, 40
 Edw., 8
 George, 54, 70
 Hugh, 68, 142
 Job, 54, 70
 John, 63
 Richard, 93, 115
 Shadrach, 9
 Thomas, 47, 64
Teagan
 Thomas, 115
Temple, 45
 Benj., 9, 58
 Benjamin, 129
 Frederick, 45
Temples
 Benjn., 145
Terrell
 Arch, 64
 Will, 83
 William, 113
Terry
 James, 32
Thelford, 19
 William, 19
Thomas, 102, 127
 David, 61
 Fredk. G., 114
 Gibble, 9, 102

 James, 6, 14, 16, 23, 31, 32, 36,
  46, 95, 109, 119, 127
 John, 5, 70, 102, 109
 Jonathan, 9
 Jos., 9
 Joseph, 5, 9
 Micajah, 139
 Saml., 53
 Sarah, 5
 Tisey, 36, 53, 54, 83, 127
 William, 9, 114, 139
Thomason
 Richard, 107
 William, 107
Thompson, 52, 143
 Allen, 96
 Benj., 9
 Benja., 93
 Benjamin, 10, 61, 77
 George, 94, 95
 Henry, 134
 Ichabod, 144
 Ichabud, 104, 110, 128, 144
 Jeremiah, 20
 John N., 134
 Swan, 6
Thomson
 Berry, 15
Thorn
 James, 9
Thornton
 Hen, 141
 Henry, 8, 30, 34
 John, 123
 Lindsay, 53
 Lindsy, 6
 Linsy, 73
 Robert, 9, 15
 Solomon, 6
 Wm., 8

Thorp
  Jos., 144
Throgmorton
  James, 41
Thrower, 73
  Jere., 63
  Jeremiah, 56, 63, 70, 82, 133
Thweatt, 92
  Drury, 132
  James, 16, 17, 29, 30, 130, 141
  John, 88
  Peterson, 66
  Uriah, 60
Thweatts
  John, 8
Tiggs
  Jas., 139
Tillman
  James, 132
  John, 115, 132
Tillmon
  John, 93
Tilman
  Frederick, 9, 27, 36
  James, 35, 57, 86
  John, 9
Tingle
  John, 123
Tison, 70, 86
  Job, 34
Tolar
  Thos., 29
Tomberlin
  James, 82
Tomlin
  James, 35
Tood
  Jacob, 75
Tool
  Eli, 6

Torry
  Alexander, 38
Trader
  Purnel, 38
  Purnell, 42
Trawick
  Francis, 88
Traywick
  Jesse, 139
Trent
  William, 45
Trice, 19
  John, 19
Triplett
  Edwin, 82
  George, 82
  Nancy, 82
  Rutha, 82
Tripp, 123
  Henry, 7
  Jno., 8
  William, 8
Trippe, 37, 40, 101
  Henry, 88
  Jas., 142
  John, 40, 74, 88
  William, 40, 119, 122
Truman
  Frederick, 75
  John, 81, 83
Tucker, 19, 21
  Frederick, 19, 50, 52, 88
  Fredk., 20
Turk
  Laban, 27
  Theodocius, 19
Turner, 108, 127, 129
  ___, 9, 126
  Archibald, 101
  Edward, 15

Henry, 37, 101, 132
John, 8, 9, 40, 61, 63, 68, 87, 99, 113, 117
Joseph, 8, 12, 13, 19, 48, 103
Joseph, Jr., 65
Larkin, 33, 86
Levin, 40
Philip, 10, 19, 39, 42, 59, 76, 83, 96, 119
Phillip, 73, 87, 131
Saml., 8, 101
Samuel, 40, 123
Thomas, 33, 114
William, 33
Twilla
  Samuel, 5
  William, 5
Tyler
  John, 115
  Thomas, 115, 132
Tyson, 101
  Job, 8
Tyus
  Lewis, 103
  Wm., 65
Vaughan, 94
  Robet., 144
  Thomas, 136
Veals
  William, 53
Veazey
  Jesse, 8, 38, 46
  Jno., 133
  John, 36
  Thos., 19
  Zebulon, 20
Vest
  John, 7
Vickars
  Thomas, 10

Vickers
  Thomas, 31, 53, 82
  Thos., 141
Vincent
  Levin, 141
Vinnington
  John, 139
Vinnon, 141
Vinson
  Elisha, 33
  John, 33
  Leavin, 137
  West, 104
Wade
  Micajah, 123
Wadsworth
  Daniel, 53
  James, Jr., 53
  William, 53
Wagnon
  Daniel, 56, 63, 90
  Thomas, 90
Walden
  Samuel, 77
Walding
  Samuel, 61
Walker, 6
  Alexander, 7
  David, 70, 109
  James, 7, 61, 93
  Jas., 77
  Jeremiah, 13, 27, 29, 58
  Reuben, 61, 77, 93
  Thomas, 70, 109
  William, 70, 109
Wallen
  Enoch, 101
Waller, 118, 129, 135
  Daniel, 122
  James, 85, 103, 112, 140

Jas., 121
Nathaniel, 6, 8, 10, 34, 46, 53, 73, 82, 86, 101, 102
Nathaniel, Jr., 67
Nathl., 123
Neubal, 33
Richard, 90
Smith, 48
William, 121, 133, 140
Wm., 103
Wamack
  Abraham, 7
  William, 7
Ward
  James, 9
Warden
  Wm., 91, 108
Warren
  Jesse, 59, 132, 140
Warthen
  Elijah, 45
  William, 12
Waters, 108
Watkins
  John, 122
  Mathew, 105
Watson
  Smith, 105
Watts
  Saml., 97
  Samuel, 15, 126
Weatherby
  Septimus, 35
Wedington
  John, 7
Weekes, 96
Weeks
  John, 58, 129
  Thomas, 4
Welch

Edward, 75
Wells
  Ben, 140
  Saml., 144
  William, 60
West
  Ephraim, 7
  Geo., 20
  Sion, 36, 79
Westmoreland
  Joseph, 17
  Reuben, 17
Whatley
  Tisdal, 5
  Willie, 9
  Wyche, 5
White, 144
  Job, 123
  John, 37, 101, 119
  Saml., 101, 123
  Samuel, 37, 71, 119
Whitehurst
  John, 13
Whitfield
  Benj., 19
  Benjamin, 34, 108
Whittenton
  Thadeus, 104
Whitting___
  Ephraim, 29
Whittington
  Aaron, 29
  Cornelius, 13, 18, 29
  Ephm., 58
  Ephraim, 88, 133
  James, 29
  Jeratt, 29
  John, 29
  Richard, 29
Wilemon

Thos., 8
Wiley
  Moses, 28, 56
Wilkens
  ___, 117
Wilkerson
  James, 61
  Jas., 64, 77
  Jno., 113
  John, 63, 64
Wilkins
  James, 107
Wilkinson, 10
  Jas., 10
  John, 131
Willey
  Wm., 66
Williams, 13, 32, 127, 137
  Benja., 102
  Burgess, 115
  Christopher, 133
  Edith, 93, 107, 129
  George, 24, 32
  Howell, 134, 140
  Jno., 133
  John, 7, 16, 109
  Thos., 33, 141
  William, 69, 70
Williamson
  John, 29
  William, 123
  Zorobabel, 7
Willis
  Burgess, 132
  James, 128
  Moses, 9
  Thomas, 57
  Thos., 7, 15, 128
  William, 7, 16, 57
Willson, 130, 134

James, 15
Wilson
  Benjamin, 134
  Isaac, 58, 131
  James, 35, 53
  Jas., 97
  John, 67, 71, 72, 76
Winslet, 73
  John, 10
Winslett, 107, 129
Wisenan
  John, 16
Wisener
  John, 53
Womack
  Abraham, 49
  Mancil, 19
  Sherwood, 19, 20
Wommack
  David, 109
  Shearwood, 90
Wood, 132
  Green, 70
  James, 23, 36, 61, 77, 93, 115
  Joseph, 115
Woodruff
  Benja., 64
Woodward
  Aaron, 4
Wooten
  James, 109
Wooton
  James, 70
Works
  James, 10
  Jas., 108
Worsham
  Anna, 74
  Betsey, 74
  Jeremiah, 100

Thomas, 39, 52
Wray
　Reuben, 17
Wright
　Demsey, 64
　Dionitious, 122
　Peter, 35
　Stephen, 109, 140
　William, 4
Wyches
　Bath, 10
Wyley
　Moses, 103
Wylie
　Moses, 88
Wynn
　Green, 109
　Joshua, 7
　Thomas, 6
　Thomas, Sr., 7

Thweatts, 81
Wynne
　Green, 65
　Greene, 90
　Joshua, 132
　Thos., 65
Yarborough, 13, 21
Yarbrough, 111, 114
　James, 95
Yarnel
　Danl., 64
Yarnell
　Aron, 64
Youngblood, 118, 127, 129
　Arthur, 13, 53, 58, 65, 108
　Isaac, 53, 139
　Jonathan, 65
　Nathan, 53
　William, 53

www.ingramcontent.com/pod-product-compliance
Lightning Source LLC
Chambersburg PA
CBHW020651300426
44112CB00007B/325